STO

LONESOME WHISTLE

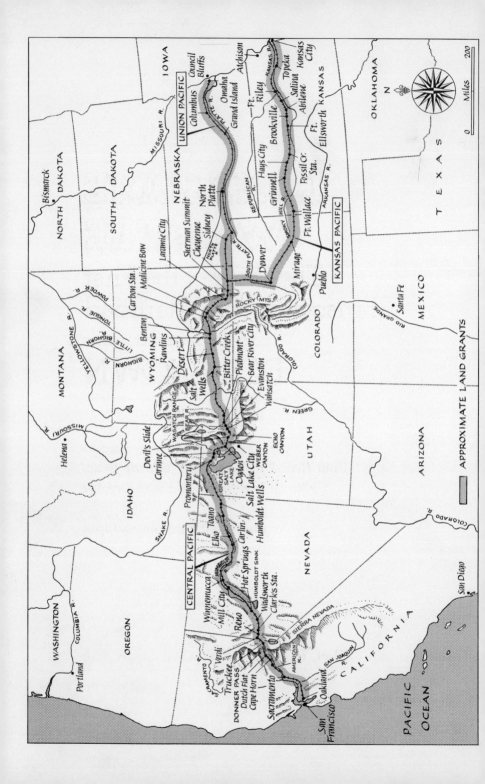

LONESOME WHISTLE

The Story of the First Transcontinental Railroad

DEE BROWN

Adapted for young readers
from *Hear That Lonesome Whistle Blow*,
with the assistance of Linda Proctor

illustrated with photographs

Holt, Rinehart and Winston / New York

Library of Congress Cataloging in Publication Data

Brown, Dee Alexander.   Lonesome whistle.

   Bibliography: p.   Includes index.
   SUMMARY: Describes the building of the first
transcontinental railroad and discusses train
travel in the West in general in the late 19th century.
1. Railroads—The West—History—Juvenile literature.
2. The West—History—Juvenile literature.
[1. Railroads—The West—History.   2. The West—History]
I. Title.   HE2763 1977.B76 1980   385′.0978
79-18990   ISBN 0-03-050666-2

Contents

2110792

LONESOME WHISTLE

1:

The Iron Horse
Crosses the Mississippi

Over a crude track near Honesdale, Pennsylvania, on August 8, 1829, the first railroad locomotive in America made its test run. Within twenty years after that run, rail lines were crossing the Alleghenies from the port cities of the East, heading toward the West. In 1852, the first locomotive steamed into Chicago.

The pioneer builder who brought that first railroad to Chicago was Henry Farnam. Born into a poor New England family, Farnam had to read his school books by the light of an open fireplace. He taught himself mathematics so as to become a surveyor, found employment in the canal business, and was soon contracting the building of canals. Farnam foresaw, however, that railroads would replace canals in importance, and he switched to building railroads. Like a number of other young railroad men, he was soon dreaming of a route across America—all the way to the Pacific Ocean.

Reaching Chicago was only the first step in Farnam's dream. The next step was to build tracks to the Mississippi River. After a thorough survey of approaches to the river, he chose the town of Rock Island for the terminus of the rails from Chicago. Always looking one step ahead, Farnam noted that in the middle of the river was an island—Rock Island—for which the town was named. Farnam's engineering knowledge told him that by using the island, he could easily build a bridge to take his railroad across the Mississippi to Iowa, and on west to another goal.

With his associates, Farnam now organized the Chicago & Rock Island Railroad and began laying tracks from Chicago toward the Mississippi River. Late in February 1854, the track layers were nearing Rock Island, and he chose February 22, Washington's Birthday, as a proper day to celebrate the final achievement.

To meet the deadline, the Chicago & Rock Island's track layers had to work overtime. While they hurriedly drove spikes into ties, another crew of workmen in Chicago was preparing a locomotive for the first run. Perhaps because of the last-minute rush, the locomotive was given no name. It was simply Locomotive No. 10, a 4-4-0 American-type engine—four small wheels up front, four big driving wheels, and no wheels under the cab.

To give Locomotive No. 10 a festive air, its crew decorated the front and sides with wreaths, garlands, and banners of red, white, and blue. Pulling six passenger cars filled with railroad officials and their guests, it came whistling into Rock Island's brand-new station in the late afternoon of Washington's Birthday. A waiting crowd greeted the arrival with cheers and waving flags.

Since its earliest days, Rock Island had been a riverboating town. Across the Mississippi on the Iowa side of the river was Davenport, many of whose people also made their living from the steamboat trade. Men who worked on the river feared the railroads because they thought this new method of transportation would take away their jobs.

Locomotive No. 10, decorated in the patriotic colors of America, stood facing the river and the West, breathing out its steam and smoke like some mythical dragon. Only a few people who were there that day gave thought to the possibility that the iron tracks which had brought a locomotive to the Mississippi would someday go all the way across Iowa to the Great Plains of Nebraska. And only the dreamers believed that railroads would ever cross the high Rockies to reach the shores of the Pacific Ocean.

In that year of 1854, travelers to California had to journey overland in wagons or stagecoaches, or take the long water route around the continent. Beyond the Mississippi River was a land of plains and mountains filled with natural resources. Its delicate balance of animals, grasses, shrubs, trees, streams, and several dozen American Indian tribes combined to create a unique environ-

On Washington's birthday, 1854, Americans celebrated the arrival of this Rock Island passenger train at the banks of the Mississippi River.

ment. As yet, white men had made little change in the Western landscape. The wagon trains and riverboats left slight traces of their passage through the vast land. Even the California gold rush had not changed the environment very much.

But now a new force from the East had reached the banks of the Mississippi, a metal monster breathing steam, a locomotive on iron tracks. When the Indians first saw this machine they called it an iron horse. Its power was recognized by an orator of the time: "The

iron horse with the wings of the wind, its nostrils distended with flame, salamander-like vomiting fire and smoke, trembling with power, but submissive to the steel curb imposed upon him by the hand of man." Before the 19th century ended, the iron horse would change the face of the American West.

On that cold, sunlit Washington's Birthday of 1854, the rejoicing passengers left the train cars to enter the spacious Rock Island station and join a banquet and celebration. A lively brass band greeted them with

"Hail, Columbia." Several toasts were made to George Washington and to other important people. After each toast, a man would signal the engineer on the iron horse outside to blow the ear-splitting whistle. The band would follow the whistle toot with its favorite march tune, "The Railroad Quickstep."

Henry Farnam was, of course, the hero of the day. When he spoke to the celebrating crowd in the station, he gave most of the credit for finishing the railroad to his associates. He expressed surprise at how fast the iron horse had crossed the eastern half of the continent. Some of his associates, all hardy young men whose ages ranged from the early twenties to the middle thirties, would become more famous during the next decade for the building of the first transcontinental railroad. These men were: Thomas Clark Durant, who was in charge of raising money for the Chicago & Rock Island Railroad; Peter Anthony Dey, engineer in charge of locating and surveying the best routes for the tracks; Grenville Mellen Dodge, Dey's assistant; and Samuel Benedict Reed, construction engineer.

Not all of Farnam's young associates were with him in Rock Island for the Washington's Birthday celebration. Dey and Dodge were busy in Iowa choosing a route farther west for the railroad. Durant was in the East trying to raise money to build tracks across Iowa, from Davenport on the Mississippi to Council Bluffs on the Missouri River. They were already thinking of changing the name of the Chicago & Rock Island to the Chicago,

Rock Island & *Pacific* Railroad. The Chicago, Rock Island & Pacific itself would never reach the Pacific Ocean, but many of the men working on it would be in the great transcontinental railroad race soon to come.

Not long after the Washington's Birthday celebration in Rock Island, Farnam organized the Railroad Bridge Company and announced that construction of a bridge across the river would soon begin. Steamboat owners in St. Louis and other cities along the Mississippi immediately protested. They claimed that the bridge would be a danger to passing vessels and should not be built. Their real worry, of course, was that the railroad might take away much of their freighting business.

Confident that a bridge could be built across the river and the island without disturbing steamboat traffic, Farnam started construction of piers and superstructure. Another group now began to protest—sectionalists from the Southern states. The Southerners wanted the first transcontinental railroad to cross the nation through their part of the country. The leader of this group in the slaveholding states was Jefferson Davis, who in 1854 was Secretary of War for the United States Government. Seven years later, at the beginning of the Civil War, Davis would become President of the Confederate States of America. Now he was trying to stop the building of the bridge by claiming that Rock Island was a military reservation and therefore should not be used in the building of such a bridge.

Meanwhile the steamboat people took their case to

court and delayed construction until July 1855, when a judge finally ruled in favor of the Railroad Bridge Company.

Nine months later, Farnam's 1,535-foot-long bridge was completed. On April 22, 1856, he was one of the passengers on the first train from the East to cross the Mississippi River. In Davenport and Rock Island, church bells rang and crowds cheered. News went by telegraph back to the cities of the East and caused much excitement. "Civilization took a railroad trip across the Mississippi," declared the *Philadelphia Bulletin*. "The great bridge over the great river . . . was completed and a train of cars passed over it, carrying a load of passengers who will always look back exultingly and boast to their children and grandchildren that they were in the first train of cars that ever crossed the Mississippi."

If Farnam and Durant believed their troubles with the Mississippi rivermen were over, they must have been surprised a few days later. Early in the morning of May 6, loud steamboat whistles and alarm bells started ringing. This noise brought the people of Rock Island and Davenport out of their houses to see smoke in the sky over the new bridge. Just after dawn, the *Effie Afton*, a packet boat from New Orleans, had crashed against the bridge. Her chimneys had been knocked down and her stoves turned over, setting the vessel on fire. Quickly the blaze spread to a wooden section of the bridge. While crowds watched, one flaming bridge span fell into the river. Both boat and span went floating away with the current.

Up and down the Mississippi that morning, steamboats blew their whistles, as though they had won a contest with the railroads. Some railroad people thought the wreck of the *Effie Afton* had not been an accident. They suspected a plot by the rivermen when the steamboat *Hamburg* raised a large banner that read: BRIDGE DESTROYED. LET ALL REJOICE.

Steamboaters now tried to have the entire bridge removed legally. Steamboat pilots and captains claimed that the structure was "a great and serious obstacle to navigation." The owner of the *Effie Afton* brought a suit against the bridge company, saying that the bridge piers had created a swift river current that made the boat crash.

To meet these charges, Farnam and his associates searched for a first-rate lawyer. They found one who was known for winning most of his cases. He lived in Springfield, Illinois, and his name was Abraham Lincoln.

Meanwhile the railroad owners ignored the steamboat men and began rebuilding the burned portion of the bridge. The structure was repaired and ready for use in September 1856.

The legal case against the railroad was a long time in coming to court. On September 1, 1857, Abraham Lincoln visited Rock Island and studied the bridge. He questioned the bridge master and several steamboat pilots and other rivermen. After carefully gathering this information, he walked out on the bridge. He sat for an hour or so, studying the currents of the river. A teenaged boy, Ben Brayton, helped him measure the speed and direction of the currents. With Lincoln's silver watch, they timed the speed of logs and brush that young Brayton dropped into the stream.

A week later the court proceedings began in the Saloon Building at Clark and Lake streets in Chicago. It was to be known as the Rock Island Bridge Case. Many people were questioned during the trial. A parade of boat owners, pilots, engineers, and bridge builders passed through the courtroom to be questioned and cross-questioned. During the first days, Lincoln spent much of his time seated on a bench whittling. But when he did rise to talk he had a fund of information about the bridge. He knew the exact length of its spans, the depth of the water, and details about the *Effie Afton*. He was also very knowledgeable about the river currents, thanks to the help of Ben Brayton.

At that time, Lincoln was in his early forties, and beardless. He spoke clearly and with logic. Although he had a solemn appearance, his frontier sense of humor won him attention. The Chicago press and men of power and influence admired his abilities. Two years later these people would push him into the race for President of the United States.

Lincoln argued that railroads had as much right to cross rivers as did steamboats. Although the jurors in the case failed to reach a decision and were dismissed by the judge, the railroad people knew that they were victorious.

Abraham Lincoln when he defended the railroads in the Rock Island Bridge Case of 1857.

(Courtesy of the Illinois State Historical Library)

In the meantime Peter Dey and his young associate, Grenville Dodge, were completing surveys for the proposed railroad route between Davenport on the Mississippi and Council Bluffs on the Missouri. The railroad that would cross this area was given a new name: the Mississippi & Missouri.

Thomas Durant, in charge of finances, believed that the only reason for building railroads was to make money. As a young man, he had graduated with honors from a medical school, but he soon became bored with medicine. He decided instead that he wanted to make money by building railroads. Yet he still liked to be called "Dr." Durant.

By the spring of 1855, Durant had assembled enough financial backing to begin grading the right-of-way for the Mississippi & Missouri Railroad across Iowa. Henry Farnam chose six hundred men at Davenport to be laborers on this project. Many of the workmen were immigrants—young men who had come to the United States from Ireland. In June 1855 they laid the first rails, and a month later the Mississippi & Missouri's first locomotive arrived. It was named Antoine Le Claire. Le Claire, a half-blood Potawatomi Indian, was one of the founders of the town of Davenport, and he had given his townhouse to the railroad to be made into a luxurious railroad station. The Antoine Le Claire was handsomely decorated; on its sides were two bronze bas-reliefs of the man for whom it was named.

A large crowd gathered to admire the new locomotive. The engineer and fireman filled its boiler with water and its tender with scrap lumber. Steam and smoke began pouring from it, and the monster came to life. The engineer invited people to climb aboard for the trial run. Some of the riders were Le Claire's Indian relatives and friends. The blankets they wore were as brightly colored as the newly painted iron horse that had invaded their land. "They swarmed upon and over her, a score of them," an observer reported, "and so, with all the passengers, red and white, that could be stuck on the tender and the cab, the first run in this section of the United States was made."

Iowans named Henry Farnam "Farnam the Railroad

King." Almost every morning he went out with his workmen, urging them to complete at least half a mile of track each day.

The people of Iowa City were so eager for railroad service that they offered the Mississippi & Missouri fifty thousand dollars if they would bring the iron horse into Iowa City before January 1, 1856. In that time, fifty thousand dollars was a large fortune, and Farnam accepted the challenge. Although rain and cold weather slowed down his track layers, he was within three miles of Iowa City on Christmas Day. The temperature was often zero or below, which made work very difficult. Ice formed in the locomotive boilers and the workmen complained of frostbite.

On New Year's Eve, the deadline was only a few hours away. The end of the track was still several hundred feet from the Iowa City depot. Farnam ordered big bonfires to be built along the railroad for warmth and light. He hired every man in Iowa City who was willing to work. The locomotive crawled to within two hundred feet of the station when its boiler froze. Farnam ordered his men to use pinch bars to move the iron horse inch by inch until it stood at the end of the track beside the station platform. A few minutes later, church bells rang to celebrate the new year of 1856. Farnam had won the race and the fifty thousand dollars.

Three days later, with the temperature still well below zero, the first passenger train rolled in from Davenport. Aboard was a huge load of fresh oysters, the first to come to the heart of Iowa. That evening, Henry Farnam spent a large part of his fifty-thousand-dollar prize on a feast for all the people of the city. He served them hot coffee, cake, and oysters all night and into the morning.

2:

The Rails Point Westward

Hannibal, Missouri, was the home of Samuel Clemens, who later became known as the writer Mark Twain. In the 1840s there were rumors around Hannibal of a railroad to be built to the west.

Hannibal was a riverboat town but railroad fever struck there also. Anybody who owned a map could see that a railroad running from Hannibal to St. Joseph on the Missouri River would cut several hundred miles off the long distance west by way of St. Louis. The town's businessmen often gathered to discuss the plan of a railroad in the office of Hannibal's justice of the peace. This man was John Clemens, Mark Twain's father.

It was not until the autumn of 1850 that the merchants and bankers of Hannibal found a way to raise enough money to build their rail system. These businessmen had decided to name it the Hannibal & St. Joseph Railroad. Congress had begun giving grants of public land to companies to build railroads. The backers of the Hannibal & St. Joseph Railroad applied and received one of these grants from Washington—several million dollars' worth of farmland.

The builders of the Hannibal & St. Joseph worked hard to reach the Missouri River. On February 13, 1859, Joseph Robidoux, the old mountain man who had founded the town of St. Joseph for the American Fur Company, drove a golden spike into the last railroad tie at Cream Ridge near Chillicothe. Now the Hannibal & St. Joseph Railroad, which had been formed in 1850, was completed.

As Rock Island had done exactly five years earlier, the town of St. Joseph postponed its celebration until Washington's Birthday. To mark the occasion of connecting two great rivers by rail, a jug of water from the Mississippi was hauled by the railroad to St. Joe. There it was ceremoniously mixed with water from the muddy Missouri. In that year, Mark Twain happened to be earning his living as a steersman on a Mississippi steamboat.

In the same year of 1859, railroad fever was also brewing in the new state of California. A thirty-three-year-old Connecticut Yankee was in the state capital of Sacramento talking to local politicians about building a railroad to the East. This man was Theodore Judah, a civil engineer who had come to California to help build a short-line railroad from Sacramento to the gold mines east of the town. While working on the short-line, Judah became fascinated with the idea of building a transcontinental railroad.

Theodore Judah was so excited about the railroad that he was nicknamed "Crazy Judah." In spite of this nickname he managed to arrange an official California railroad convention; it was held in San Francisco in October 1859. Businessmen at the convention who had invested money in stagecoaches and steamboats laughed at Judah's belief that a railroad could be built across the rugged Sierra Nevada mountains. But Judah described a route through this range that would continue eastward by way of the California overland trail. After passing through the Rockies the railroad would follow the Platte River to Omaha and Council Bluffs. The skeptical delegates at the railroad convention finally agreed to send Judah to Washington. There he would do his best to obtain government support for a transcontinental railroad.

In 1859, however, the Hannibal & St. Joseph seemed a more likely government choice for the first link in a railroad across the West. The Hannibal & St. Joseph was the only completed rail route to the stagecoach towns along the Missouri River, and its passenger and freight traffic had already proven to be successful. In the spring of the following year, the Hannibal & St. Joseph's hopes became greater when Pony Express mail service to California began at the town of St. Joseph.

At about noon on April 3, 1860, a special messenger carrying mail from New York, Washington, and other Eastern cities crossed the Mississippi River on a ferryboat. The messenger then boarded a special train on the Hannibal & St. Joseph. That day the engineer on the train set a record that was not beaten for fifty years. He brought the messenger into St. Joe in less than five hours. They were just in time to transfer the mail to the saddlebags of Johnny Frey, the first Pony Express rider. Flags were flying, bands were playing, and crowds were cheering. A cannon boomed and jockey-sized Johnny Frey leaped into his saddle and galloped for the ferry that would take him across the Missouri. From there he would begin the long 1,996-mile run to California.

"Hardly will the cloud of dust which envelops the rider die away," said St. Joseph's mayor Jeff Thompson, "before the puff of steam will be seen on the horizon." The directors of the railroad in St. Joe were so sure that they would soon be hauling mail all the way to California by rail that they ordered the building of the first post-office car. In this car, mail could then be sorted and bagged while it traveled.

In the meantime, "Crazy Judah" had not been successful in Washington. He left the East to return to California, still determined to build a transcontinental railroad. Without government support, however, he would have to seek funds from the public, and he knew that he could not obtain money from practical businessmen unless he could prove that the railroad was worthwhile.

Meanwhile the American Civil War had begun in the East. Disregarding the distant battles, Judah spent the summer mapping a route through the Sierras. He hoped his route would convince businessmen that the iron horse could successfully cross the Sierra Nevada mountains. His route would take the rails from Dutch Flat through Donner Pass and the Truckee River Canyon, and then down to the Washoe gold country of Nevada. The discovery of Nevada gold and silver, the fabulous Comstock lode, helped attract Sacramento's business leaders to Judah's railroad dream. The earlier gold rush in California had made these men wealthy. Now that the California gold rush was coming to an end, they were looking for opportunities to make more money in the booming Nevada towns. Even if Judah's railroad was never completed, a wagon road for use in its construction would have to be built across the mountains. Whoever owned that highway would control transportation in and out of Nevada.

Whatever their reasons might be, "Crazy Judah" needed the support of these men in Sacramento. Some of the merchants who joined him in his railroad scheme were: Leland Stanford, owner of a wholesale grocery business, who planned to run for governor as a candidate of Abraham Lincoln's new political party, the Republicans; Collis P. Huntington and Mark Hopkins, who had started a miner's supply store in a small tent in Sacramento and had built it into the largest hardware enterprise on the Pacific Coast; and Charlie Crocker, who owned a dry-goods store. Others were jewelers, owners of mines, and traders of various sorts. But of all those involved with the railroad, these were the Big Four: Stanford, Huntington, Hopkins, and Crocker. Together with Judah they incorporated the Central Pacific Railroad in California on June 28, 1861.

Judah returned to Washington as an agent of the Central Pacific to make a second attempt to obtain money from the government. He discovered that other railroad forces were also hard at work on Capitol Hill for the same purposes. In response to these lobbyists, the U. S. Congress proposed that a transcontinental railroad be built by two companies. One would lay tracks from the Pacific Coast to the eastern border of California. The other would build westward across the Plains and the Rockies to link up with the tracks of the California railroad.

Men from the Hannibal & St. Joseph were in Washington, urging that their railroad be chosen to build westward to the California border. But the most active group was headed by James C. Stone, president of the Leavenworth, Pawnee & Western Railroad Company.

Had it not been for the Civil War, the Leavenworth railroad or the Hannibal & St. Joseph probably would have been Congress' choice for the first link in a transcontinental railroad. Unfortunately for these companies, the Civil War was causing them trouble. Confederate soldiers were raiding the Missouri railroads, wrecking trains, blowing up bridges, and capturing trainmen. The Rebels even kidnapped the president of the Hannibal & St. Joseph, threatening to shoot him unless he halted train service. The Leavenworth rail system was also in border territory between the North and the South. That made it a possible target for raids by William Quantrill, Sterling Price, and other Confederate cavalry leaders.

By the spring of 1862, it became obvious to Congress that the road would have to be built farther north. In Congress' final decision, the railroad to be constructed from the East was given a name: Union Pacific Railroad Company. It was to build "a single line of railroad and telegraph from a point to be fixed by the President of the United States." After having finished forty consecutive miles, this railroad would be given land grants and bonds from the government. In the same act of Congress, the other major railroad company, the Central Pacific, was given the right to construct rails from the Pacific Coast to the eastern boundary of California. The terms and conditions were the same for the two roads— which meant both would receive enormous land grants.

3:

The Race Begins

Shortly after President Lincoln signed the transcontinental railroad bill into law, Huntington and Judah moved the headquarters of the Central Pacific to New York. From there they ordered rails and locomotives to be sent by sea to California. It was difficult to obtain iron in the years of the Civil War. Much of it was being used for guns and other military equipment.

In spite of this difficulty, the Central Pacific was able to ship enough supplies to start building. By the end of the year, the Central Pacific announced that groundbreaking ceremonies would be held at Sacramento on January 8, 1863.

On that morning, heavy rain muddied the streets, but before noon the sun was shining brightly. A group of carriages rolled through the streets, their wheels muddy to the hubs. They were decorated with patriotic bunting, in the colors of red, white, and blue. Bales of hay were spread on the street to prevent the crowd from sinking into the mud while listening to the speeches.

To keep their long skirts out of the muck, many of the women watched the celebration from the balcony of a nearby hotel. Taking refuge on the same balcony was a local brass band which began the ceremonies by playing "Wait for the Wagon." Two flag-covered wagons were pulled up before the platform. One of them displayed a banner with a picture of two hands clasped across the United States; on the banner was written: MAY THE BOND BE ETERNAL.

After the local minister began the festivities, Charlie Crocker, the former dry-goods merchant, rose to begin the speechmaking. Crocker now called himself the superintendent of the Central Pacific Railroad. He was a big man, weighing more than 250 pounds, with a loud voice that could bellow like a bull. At high noon, he introduced the president of the Central Pacific, Leland Stanford, who had become governor of California. In contrast to Crocker, Stanford was dignified, dressed in a frock coat and high silk hat. He promised the crowd at Sacramento that the Pacific and Atlantic coasts would soon be bound by the iron bonds of the rails of the Central Pacific Railroad.

One of the plans for the day was for the governor to dig up the first spadeful of dirt that would start construction of the railroad. Because of the straw-covered mud, this was an impossible feat. However, someone had thoughtfully loaded a tubful of dry dirt into one of

the wagons. Stanford carefully leaned from the platform
and lifted out a spadeful. "Nine cheers," shouted Charlie Crocker, and the crowd yelled and applauded.

"Everybody felt happy," reported a local newspaper,
"because after so many years of dreaming, scheming,
talking and toiling, they saw with their own eyes the
actual commencement of a Pacific railroad."

It was somewhat strange that the man whose dreams
and schemes which had led to this happy celebration
was not present on that day. He was in the East, on one
of his long trips by sea and isthmus, attempting to obtain
enough credit and iron to get the railroad built. A few
months later, as he was crossing through the Panama
jungles, a mosquito bit him, and on November 2, 1863,
Theodore Judah died of yellow fever. Now his railroad
dream lay completely in the hands of the Big Four—
Stanford, Huntington, Crocker, and Hopkins.

Meanwhile in the East, the Union Pacific Railroad
was off to a much slower start. The bitter Civil War was
closer at hand for them than for the Central Pacific. In
addition, the Union Pacific was not as well organized as
the Central Pacific. There was no Big Four to control
the Union Pacific. One of several ambitious men seeking
this control was Thomas Durant. He had not been present at the original Union Pacific meetings in Chicago in
1862, but by late in 1863, Durant was scheming to gain
control of the company. As he gradually gained power
by buying up Union Pacific stock, another man moved
into his orbit. This new associate was George Francis
Train, a rather unusual man. Train had made a fortune

in shipping and railroads and was in England when the Civil War brought him back to America to help save the Union. He was in his early thirties when he met Durant, and he immediately became enthusiastic about the idea of a transcontinental railroad.

Train and Durant had very different personalities. Durant liked to make money and he worked patiently to get it, like a spider weaving webs to catch flies. Train thought little of money except for the fun it could bring; he was an energetic, impatient person with a zest for life.

Train could not understand the slowness of the Union Pacific in getting construction under way at Omaha, the place designated by President Lincoln for starting the railroad westward. After all, almost a year had passed since the Central Pacific had broken ground at Sacramento. Their builders were already laying track toward the Sierras.

At last, the impatient Train was able to talk Durant into starting ground-breaking ceremonies at Omaha. On December 2, 1863, two miles south of the ferry landing at Council Bluffs, several hundred people gathered. The governor of Nebraska and two companies of artillery were present to hear Train deliver one of his fiery speeches. "The great Pacific railway is commenced," he cried, "at the entrance of a garden seven hundred miles in length and twenty broad. The Pacific railroad is the nation and the nation is the Pacific railway. This is the grandest enterprise under God!"

In Omaha with Train was Peter Dey, the engineer

who had run surveys for the westward-pointed railway across Illinois and Iowa. After the governor had turned a spadeful of earth, Dey read messages from Durant and from President Lincoln. The crowd cheered and the artillery companies fired salutes to this great occasion for the Union Pacific.

Train returned to New York, certain that the building of the railroad would begin by spring. A few weeks later, Dey was appointed chief engineer of the Union Pacific. As soon as the Nebraska mud dried out in the spring, he assembled a small gang of workmen. They began grading land for a few miles straight westward from Omaha.

In 1864 the war was going badly for the Union. The armies were suffering their last great bloodbaths before the end. Because of a lack of money, Durant went to Washington to seek funds. Train was impatient with the delay. He visited Omaha occasionally, and at one point he built a new hotel because he did not like the one that was there. He casually bought some cheap Omaha real estate, which like everything else he touched rapidly turned into millions of dollars.

At last the war ended and hordes of young soldiers found themselves cut loose in a changed America. Thousands of them were immigrants who had moved to America from countries such as Ireland, Germany, and Sweden; thousands were former slaves, wandering westward in their first journeys of freedom; thousands were Confederates, the losers of the war. They were all strong, muscular men accustomed to hardships and danger, accustomed to taking orders.

Late in 1865, only a few months after the war's end, steamboats as numerous as wild geese were pushing up the Missouri River toward Omaha. (The railroads in Iowa were still months away from reaching the Missouri.) Some of the boats were loaded with iron rails, locomotives, shovels, plows, spikes. Others carried passengers, mostly young men heading westward, looking for work. These boats were going to Omaha, a frontier village of trading posts and grog shops, a village that would soon be changing into a boom town. Omaha would be the nation's center until parallel rails of iron stretched farther, all the way across the continent.

4

Drill, Ye Tarriers, Drill

Among those who came to Omaha was Colonel Silas Seymour. He was sent by Dr. Durant to inspect the twenty-three miles of grading completed by chief engineer Peter Dey. Seymour dressed more like a dandy from the city than a working railroad man. He wore fancy clothing and kept a well-trimmed goatee. He told Dey that Dr. Durant had appointed him "consulting engineer" of the Union Pacific, and that he was ready to begin work.

As Mr. Dey was soon to discover, Colonel Seymour was a difficult man to work with. Soon after he began his duties as the Union Pacific's "consulting engineer," Seymour made changes in the route. Dey had already planned the route west of Omaha, and had graded the roadbed. Seymour's plan required nine more miles of track, and Dey refused to agree to the changes. His own route was a direct line, whereas Seymour's was longer.

Omaha as it looked when the Union Pacific began building westward.   *(Photo by A. J. Russell,*
        Courtesy of The Oakland Museum History Department)

Dey could see that Seymour had planned the longer passage in order to obtain more money from the government. Seymour's route would also acquire more of the valuable land close to the growing city of Omaha. Dey believed that railroad routes should be as short as possible. When he refused Seymour's proposal Dey resigned as chief engineer.

Durant never admitted that he received a letter of resignation from Dey. He simply told Colonel Seymour to act as chief engineer of the Union Pacific. Although Seymour had some experience, he actually knew very little about railroad construction. For example, he still believed that parallel timbers made better supports for rails than cross ties. When he was ordered to use cross ties, he bought cheap cottonwood, instead of sturdier hardwood. After discovering how quickly cottonwood rotted, he invested thousands of dollars in a wood-preservation device that did not work very well.

Samuel B. Reed, who had worked with Dey on the railroads out of Chicago, directed most of the surveying for Seymour's new route. Reed soon realized how out of place Seymour was at the railroad-building site. Even the Pawnee Indians laughed at him as he rode out on horseback to inspect the road. He must have looked odd to them, wearing a black silk top hat and carrying an umbrella to protect himself from the summer sun.

Seymour's crew did not lay the first rail on their road bed until July 10, 1866. The fastest they could cross the flat prairie was one mile of track per week. In October, when Durant visited Omaha with General William

Tecumseh Sherman to try to speed up construction, only fifteen miles of track had been completed. Money was running short and more miles of track were needed to claim more government funds. Inviting Sherman to Omaha was probably George Francis Train's idea. As a Civil War hero, Sherman received attention from the press wherever he went. He brought the Union Pacific the publicity they were in dire need of, to sell stock and obtain more funds.

To please Sherman, the men painted his name in shiny letters on Union Pacific Locomotive No. 1. Passenger cars had not yet been brought up the Missouri, so a platform car was attached to the iron horse with seats made from boards fastened to upside-down kegs. Sherman, Durant, Train, and a dozen or so other men wrapped themselves in buffalo robes and took a ride for the fifteen miles to the end of the track. There at Sailing's Grove, they had a picnic of roast duck and champagne.

Before Sherman left Omaha there were probably talks among the men about the problems of finances. Durant was aware of the fact that the Union Pacific might lose its funds for the transcontinental railway if one of the Kansas railroads reached the 100th meridian first. The 100th meridian was only a line on the map of America, running north and south across the plains of Nebraska and Kansas. But it symbolized the heart of the young nation, a dividing line midpoint between East and West. A race to cross it now began.

That autumn, the old Leavenworth railroad, which

had changed its name to Union Pacific, Eastern Division, completed sixty miles of track. Its work crews were reported to be laying a mile of track each day. Durant knew that if the Kansas railroad reached the 100th meridian before his company, the government might give the railroad from Kansas the right to continue building to California.

Durant quickly realized that Colonel Seymour, although a good friend, lacked the drive to win the 257-mile race to the 100th meridian. A new engineer had to be found, and General Sherman recommended thirty-five-year-old Grenville Dodge, who had been one of Sherman's most dependable officers during the Georgia campaign of the Civil War. Durant followed Sherman's advice and persuaded Dodge to leave the Army and report for railroad duty in May 1866.

In the meantime, Durant also employed another former Civil War leader, John S. Casement. Casement had commanded a division in the U. S. Army, and was from Sherman's home state of Ohio. He had worked as a track hand in Michigan and was then foreman of a track-building gang in Ohio. In the spring of 1866, Jack Casement and his brother Dan arrived in Omaha to work for Durant. Standing in his laced boots, Jack Casement reached only five foot four. His brother Dan was even shorter, "five foot nothing." They looked like a pair of bearded midgets but were soon to be called "the biggest little men you ever saw." Adam Schoup, who worked as personal wagoner for Jack Casement, said he "never saw a man you worked harder for. Many times we drove twenty-four hours, changing horses, and when I played out, Jack drove."

From the swarms of men coming west up the Missouri, the Casements hired about a thousand of the strongest. Many were Irish, and many were American-born veterans of the Union and Confederate armies. Several were former Negro slaves. To fill out the ranks, General Dodge suggested using captured Indians to do the grading, the Army furnishing "a guard to make the Indians work, and to keep them from running away." But the men building the railroad did not like his idea of making slaves of red men. After all, many of them had just spent four years fighting a war to free four million black slaves.

It was difficult to add to a track that stretched for hundreds of miles into mostly uninhabited country. The Casement brothers solved this problem with the invention of the "work train." It was simply a short train, with about a dozen cars attached behind an iron horse. Each car had a special purpose on the work train.

One was filled with tools, and one was a blacksmith shop. Another was a kitchen with rough dining tables and a supply of food. Others had built-in bunks. At the end were several flatcars loaded with rails, spikes, fish-plates, bolts, and other railroad-building supplies. The train was like a small town on wheels.

After General Dodge came to Omaha in May, the building of the Union Pacific became much like a mili-

tary campaign. A newspaper reporter described the surveyors and locators as the "advance guard," and the
graders as the "second line, cutting through the gorges,
grading the road and building the bridges. Then comes
the main body of the army, placing the ties, laying the
track, spiking down the rails, perfecting the alignment,
ballasting and dressing up and completing the road for
immediate use. Along the line of the completed road are
construction trains pushing 'to the front' with supplies.
The advance limit of the rails is occupied by a train of
long box-cars with bunks built within them, in which
the men sleep at night and take their meals." He continued to describe the activities of the tracklayers, the
gaugers, the spikers, and the bolters.

Jack and Dan Casement set a goal of one mile of track
to be laid each day. They offered each man in the work
crew a pound of tobacco if a mile of track was laid
between sunup and sundown. When they reached that
goal, the Casements offered three dollars per day instead of the regular two dollars if the men could lay a
mile and a half. And then as the workmen sweated
under the midsummer sun, the Casements promised to
pay four dollars for laying two miles a day.

Like most outdoor laboring men, the tracklayers
often sang while they worked, sometimes making up
their own songs. Perhaps the rhythm of tracklaying
helped them create these songs. The track boss commanded, "Down," "Down," every thirty seconds to signal the dropping of the rails into place. "They were the

pendulum beats of a mighty era," a newspaperman wrote. "They marked the time of the march and its regulation step."

While working, the spike drivers let out their breath in a deep-sounding rhythm, in time to their sledgehammers. Suited to this rhythm was "Drill, my Paddies, drill. Drill all day, No sugar in your tay, Workin' on the U. P. Railway." Although it was twenty years later before this song was set to music, it was more closely associated with the building of the Union Pacific than any other song:

> Drill, ye tarriers, drill.
> Drill, ye tarriers, drill,
> Oh, it's work all day
> No sugar in your tay,
> Workin' on the U. Pay Ra-ailway!

By August 1, the work train was 150 miles west of Omaha, and more laborers were added to the payroll. As the nights grew colder, Casement supplied the men with tents. Every night the "tent city" moved another mile or two across the plains of Nebraska.

Early in that summer of 1866, the Union Pacific was given another reason to speed construction. Congress changed the Pacific Railway Act, allowing the Central Pacific to build farther east of the California-Nevada border. From now on, the meeting of the two railroads would depend on how fast each could build its tracks.

Grading crews finishing off a roadbed after the tracklayers have
moved on.   *(F. Jay Haynes photo-Haynes Foundation)*

The news came like a pistol shot signaling the start of a
race across the continent. The Union Pacific employed
more graders, who worked fifty to a hundred miles
ahead of the tracklayers. General Dodge packed his
surveying instruments, and he and Sam Reed headed for
Wyoming. There they would choose the final route
through the Rockies.

The Casement brothers easily won the 247-mile race
to the 100th meridian on October 5, 1866. Durant,
Train, and Seymour began planning a grand trip to that
point on the Nebraska plain. They sent invitations to
President Andrew Johnson and members of his Cabinet,
to all members of Congress, and to foreign ambassadors.
More important to Durant, they invited men of wealth
who might invest money in the railroad. "No railroad

excursion of similar character and magnitude," Colonel Seymour bragged, "had ever been projected in this or any other country."

President Johnson did not accept the invitation. He was growing suspicious of what he called "the railroad aristocracy." But more than two hundred of the nation's richest and most powerful men and women did travel to Omaha. Present to record the events were a corps of newspapermen and a photographer. Colonel Seymour was a gourmet cook, and he made plans for special meals for the receptions and balls at Omaha. The menus included boiled trout à la Normande, leg of mutton with caper sauce, quails on toast, buffalo tongue, escalloped oysters Louisiana style, antelope with sauce bigarde, braised bear in port wine sauce, grouse in Madeira sauce, and teal ducks à la royale.

For the rail journey from Omaha to the 100th meridian, the travelers boarded four brand-new passenger coaches. They were given the use of a saloon car with a bar, a mess car for meals, the Union Pacific directors' car, and Dr. Durant's private car. His private car had been President Lincoln's official car during the Civil War. Durant acquired it after it was used to carry the assassinated President's body from Washington to be buried in Springfield, Illinois. The car was said to have sheets of boiler-plate metal inside its walls to stop rifle bullets.

The party of people traveling to the 100th meridian stopped at Columbus, Nebraska, for the night. They stayed in a luxurious tent camp furnished with mattresses, buffalo robes, and blankets. By the light of campfires and a harvest moon they watched a band of Pawnees perform a war dance. The next morning the train rolled onto the fifteen-hundred-foot Loup Fork bridge, where the Pawnees again entertained the travelers. Riding horses, the Indians performed in a mock battle. Afterward, Dr. Durant paid off the Pawnee actors with the usual presents of baubles and gimcracks. The guests watching did not know that the Pawnees had earlier forced Durant to pay a hundred dollars cash down before they would perform. These Indians had been dealing with white men going west for a long time. They knew that white men's promises meant very little. And they knew the value of white men's money.

When the travelers reached the 100th meridian, they found no tracklayers at work. There was only a wide arched sign that read: 100TH MERIDIAN, 247 MILES FROM OMAHA. The Casement brothers and their "tarriers" had moved on another twenty-two miles west. Eager to show his guests how a railroad was built, Durant took them on to the end of the track, where they watched the sweating workmen until sundown. The men took a break only once to pose for a photograph made by Professor John Carbutt. At dusk the workmen retired to their simple tent camp to dine on beans and fatback. Meanwhile, the travelers in their luxurious camp area were eating lamb with green peas, roasted antelope, and Chinese duck, all washed down with champagne.

After dinner Colonel Seymour put on a fireworks display, and the travelers watched rockets, exploding stars, and pinwheels until bedtime. Those track builders who were not too tired to stay awake also watched this heavenly spectacle.

On the trip back to Omaha the next morning, the train halted beside the arched 100th meridian sign. For an hour the Very Important People and their wives posed for photographs.

The group returned to Omaha late that evening. Colonel Seymour boasted that the excursion was "the most important and successful celebration of the kind that has ever been attempted in the world." The other directors of the Union Pacific were also pleased with the grand trip. They hoped it would help them raise money. After the return of the wealthy men and politicians to the East, the nation became very interested in the Union Pacific. Millions of dollars in bonds were soon sold to benefit the railroad. Many important newspapers began sending correspondents out to the Great Plains to write about the construction work. These journalists were treated like visiting royalty by the railroad's spokesmen.

Late in November the Casement brothers ordered their men into winter quarters. Blizzard season would soon come to the Plains, and the construction crew of more than two thousand men built a tent city for protection. This temporary city was located near the meeting place of the North and South Platte rivers, and was named North Platte. The only permanent building at North Platte, 290 miles west of Omaha, was the railroad station. But because it was at the end of the track, North Platte immediately became the main point for overland stage traffic to the West. This through traffic included Mormons headed for Utah, soldiers and gold seekers, and settlers waiting for stagecoaches. Protected under mounds of sailcloth, piles of freight also waited for wagon trains.

Within a few weeks, a hundred buildings sprang up in North Platte, including hotels, warehouses, and saloons. It became one of the first of the wild, rip-roaring railroad towns, called hell-on-wheels towns, which would follow the tracks to the West. Gamblers, saloonkeepers, and other camp followers came to North Platte.

"The larger part of the floating population is made up of desperadoes," reported one newsman, "who spend their time in gambling of all kinds, from cards to keno and faro. Day and night the saloons are in full blast, and sums of money varying from five dollars to fifty and even one hundred change hands with a rapidity astonishing to one who is not accustomed to the recklessness which their wild frontier life invariably begets." A traveler passing through North Platte that winter said, "Law is unknown here," and added that some of the folks there ". . . were having a good time gambling, drinking, and shooting each other."

In the following spring, a reporter for the *Missouri Democrat* stepped off the train at North Platte. His name was Henry Morton Stanley, and he found the town in a lively uproar. "Every gambler in the Union seems to have steered his course for North Platte, and every known game under the sun is played here. The days of Pike's Peak and California are revived. Every house is a saloon, and every saloon is a gambling den. Revolvers are in great requisition. Beardless youths imitate to the life the peculiar swagger of the devil-may-care bull-whacker and blackleg . . . On account of the immense freighting done to Idaho, Montana, Utah, Dakota, and Colorado, hundreds of bull-whackers walk about, and turn the one street into a perfect Babel. Old gamblers who reveled in the glorious days of 'flush times' in the gold districts, declare that this town outstrips all yet."

Although the tracklayers moved into winter quarters in November, they continued to lay rails when weather permitted. At year's end, Jack Casement reported that the track reached to Milepost 305. Meanwhile in California, the Central Pacific was moving slower. It had not had the help of the press that the Union Pacific had in the East. The Central Pacific seemed to be playing the role of the tortoise in the race with the harelike Union Pacific. On the day that the Union Pacific laid its first rail at Omaha (July 10, 1865), the California railroad was still fifty miles out of Sacramento.

High on the western slope of the Sierras, the Central Pacific was building an advance camp at Cisco. Sacramento lay below them at thirty feet above sea level.

Cisco was almost six thousand feet higher. This extreme difference in height made it difficult for the graders, bridge builders, and tunnelers to work very quickly. They faced the problem of bringing the iron horse to the seven-thousand-foot elevation of the Sierra Nevada summit before it could go down to the Nevada plateau.

Another major problem for the Central Pacific was a shortage of workmen. Most Californians could earn more than the two or three dollars per day that the railroad offered. And new arrivals from the East wanted to seek their fortunes in gold and silver mines rather than work for the railroads. The general superintendent of the Central Pacific, oxlike Charlie Crocker, searched extensively for laborers. He finally thought of hiring some Chinese from San Francisco. James Strobridge, the man in charge of construction, however, did not like the plan. Crocker pointed out to him that Chinese laborers would work for thirty-five dollars a month, much cheaper than other workers. Strobridge, an energetic Irishman from Vermont, was worried that the Chinese were not strong enough to move earth and stone and dig tunnels. He thought they ate nothing but rice and were weak. "Did they not build the Chinese Wall," Crocker shouted, "the biggest piece of masonry in the world?" Strobridge admitted that they had done so. "All right," he said, "let's hire fifty Chinese on a trial basis. If they can't cut the mustard, that's it."

After Strobridge had worked the first gang of Chinese for a long twelve-hour day, he asked Crocker to send

More workmen arriving from China to build the Central Pacific.
*(Picture Collection, The Branch Libraries,
The New York Public Library)*

him fifty more. Within a few weeks they were hiring
every Chinese male they could find. Strobridge, who
was not easy to please, said the Chinese were the best
workers in the world. "They learn quickly, do not fight,
have no strikes that amount to anything, and are very
cleanly in their habits. They will gamble, and do quarrel
among themselves most noisily—but harmlessly." At the
end of 1865, the Central Pacific had employed almost
every able-bodied Chinese in California. The railroad's
president, Leland Stanford, then began importing fifteen thousand more from China.

Although the Chinese were popular with the owners
of the Central Pacific they were disliked by other workers. Many of the men would throw down their tools and
walk away at the sight of the Chinese dressed in their

neat blue-dyed cotton clothing and umbrella-shaped basket hats. The Central Pacific continued to employ them, however. In the summer of 1865 a newspaperman reported that nine tenths of the men at work on the railroad were Chinese, and that five thousand more were soon to be hired.

Because the Central Pacific was so far west, it was difficult for politicians, important men of wealth, and newspapermen from the East to travel there. The Union Pacific, being closer to the East, received more publicity. Crocker and Strobridge must have read some of the newspaper accounts. They began driving the Central Pacific workmen as hard as the Casement brothers were driving the men of the Union Pacific. Each railroad was determined to build tracks faster than the other. Somewhere in the West they would reach a meeting point.

While the Chinese were rolling tons of earth and stone in wheelbarrows to build embankments, and chipping away at the granite rock to build tunnels, the Big Four began worrying over the slow progress of their Central Pacific through the Sierra Mountains. In the autumn of 1865, the Union Pacific was leaping a mile a day across the level Plains. The Central Pacific moved much slower, climbing yard by yard toward snow-clad mountain summits. In November, the Central Pacific reached Cisco, ninety-two miles from Sacramento. Strobridge wanted to work through the winter building tunnels. He hauled hundreds of Chinese a dozen miles

In May 1866 the Central Pacific completed this long, curved tres-
tle near Secrettown in the Sierra Nevadas.

(Photo by A. J. Russell,
Courtesy of The Oakland Museum History Department)

up the wagon road, and put them to work digging, blasting, and hauling away rock to build the Summit Tunnel. This tunnel was to run a quarter of a mile through the stoney heart of the last mountain in the range.

To mark the new year of 1867, the *Sacramento Union* reported that the Central Pacific had a daily run to Cisco, "5,911 feet above the level of the sea—a higher altitude than is attained by any other railroad in America . . ."

Because of the snows of the Sierras and the blizzards of the Great Plains, the race was slowed down that winter. In the spring of 1868, the race would start again. Already it had become the greatest engineering and construction effort ever made in America.

5:

The Great Race

During the spring of 1868, the great race between the builders of the Union Pacific and Central Pacific railroads began in earnest. The crossing of the Sierras was an amazing accomplishment for the Central Pacific. For several months during 1867 the Central Pacific's construction superintendent, James Strobridge, had kept eight thousand Chinese tunnelers working in around-the-clock shifts seven days a week. The mountain barrier was dangerous in the winter months, and snowdrifts and avalanches made work especially precarious. This was the same mountain barrier that had tragically stopped the Donner party from the East twenty years earlier. Those California-bound emigrants had resorted to cannibalism before rescuers reached them.

To gain mileage in the race with the Union Pacific, the Big Four of the Central Pacific sent graders and tracklayers far ahead of the unfinished tunnels. Because

One of the deep cuts made by Central Pacific workmen for the crossing of the Sierras, at Owl Gap, eighty miles east of Sacramento.
(Photo by A. J. Russell,
Courtesy of The Oakland Museum History Department)

tunnel blasting was slow work, the Big Four decided they must lay rails down the eastern slope of the mountains while the tunnels were being completed. The sooner the Central Pacific tracks reached the level Nevada desert, the better chance they would have to beat the Union Pacific into Utah and Salt Lake City.

To accomplish this, Strobridge took three thousand Chinese over the summit to grade and bridge the eastern slope to the Nevada line. The greatest feat of all was when they moved three locomotives and forty cars over the mountain summit. The heavy equipment had to be dismantled and carried over on sleighs. This was no small feat because of the sliding and sinking into snow.

"We hauled locomotives over," general manager Crocker later recalled, "and when I say we, I mean myself. We hauled them on sleighs . . . we hauled some of them over on logs, because we could not get a sleigh big enough." After the iron horses and their tenders and cars were brought slipping and sliding down the slope, they had to be loaded onto wagons at Donner Lake. The wagons were dragged along a rough and muddy road to Truckee. A cavalcade of sleds and wagons followed them, with tons of spikes, plows, tools, food supplies, sawmills, and iron rails—enough to lay fifty miles of track.

While grading crews and tracklayers worked on the eastern slope, the digging of the bypassed tunnels continued. Summit Tunnel was completed and ready for the tracklayers in November; the Central Pacific had reached its highest point, 7, 017 feet above sea level. A month later, to celebrate their triumph, the Big Four loaded ten bright yellow passenger cars at Sacramento with seven hundred Very Important People of California. They hauled them up the 105-mile track to the top of the Sierras, where they had a snowball fight.

On December 13, Strobridge and his Chinese workers on the eastern slope of the range laid the first rails across the Nevada line. By the spring of 1868, they had begun grading across the arid flatlands. They moved toward

Tracklayers on the Central Pacific moving eastward across Nevada. *(Utah State Historical Society)*

the Great Basin of Utah, the green and fruitful country of the Mormons. Control of this country would be a rich prize for whichever railroad reached it first. The Big Four wanted to win it so badly that they sent teams of men to survey as far east as Wyoming. They were surprised to find eager Union Pacific surveyors there already at work.

Early that spring, the Central Pacific tracklayers reached the new town of Reno. The town, located near the Nevada mines, had been named for General Jesse L. Reno, a famous Civil War hero. The town was growing so fast that twenty-five-foot storefront lots were soon selling for twelve hundred dollars. As soon as the Central Pacific station was built, James Strobridge sent his crews back into the Sierras, where the snows were now melting. Their mission was to complete a seven-mile gap between Reno and Sacramento, after which the Big Four could collect money from the government. By mid-June the frozen earth and the large stones had been blasted and leveled; the rails had been spiked down and the gap finally closed. The Big Four could now collect a fortune from the government.

One of the passengers on the first train to cross the Sierras from Sacramento was a newspaper reporter. He described the Central Pacific Railroad as "one of the most beautiful, smooth and solid roads on the continent." He added that soon the Chinese would be crossing the mountains to the Great Basin where they would continue construction for the Central Pacific.

The president of that company, Leland Stanford, also traveled across the mountains that summer. His mission was to talk with Brigham Young in Salt Lake City. Stanford hoped that Young and other Mormon leaders would agree with his plan to build a road grade across Utah through Weber Canyon to the Wyoming line.

Young already had another agreement with the Union Pacific, but this previous agreement did not seem to bother him or the Big Four. Young saw no conflict in taking on two contracts with two railroads, especially after Stanford promised to pay the Mormons double the wages he had been giving his Chinese workers. This money came from the nation's taxpayers, most of whom were unaware that during the autumn of 1868 they were paying for two railroads to be built side by side. Two separate crews of Mormons were hard at work laying two hundred miles of parallel road grades, of which one would never be used. The great race was becoming wasteful and expensive. Yet most Americans were enthusiastic with the progress of what they thought of as "their" transcontinental railroad.

Indian attacks had been a source of danger for the Union Pacific when it had crossed the Great Plains. During the Army's campaigns against the Indians along the Kansas Pacific Railroad in 1867, a number of Indian raiders had shifted their attacks northward to the Union Pacific in Nebraska. A legendary train ambush occurred against the Union Pacific at Plum Creek on August 6. Long afterward, a Cheyenne named Porcupine told why they had wrecked the train: "The soldiers had defeated us and taken everything that we had and made us poor. We were feeling angry and said among ourselves that we ought to do something. In these big wagons that go on this metal road, there must be things that are valuable—perhaps clothing. If we could throw these wagons off the iron they run on and break them open, we should find out what was in them and could take whatever might be useful to us."

The day after the wreck occurred, reporter Henry M.

Stanley, who happened to be in Omaha, interviewed a fellow Englishman who was a survivor of the ambush. He was William Thompson, who worked as a telegraph repairman on the Union Pacific. Thompson and four other men had been sent out after nightfall on a handcar from Plum Creek to find and repair a break in the telegraph line. They did not know that the wire had been torn down by Porcupine and the other Cheyennes. The Indians had used part of the wire to fasten a railroad tie to the track. The tie was meant to derail an iron horse, but instead the handcar carrying the telegraph repairmen struck it and the Indians rose up out of the high grass to surround the men.

Four of the five repairmen were quickly killed and Thompson was shot in the arm, knocked to the ground, and scalped. Although the pain was incredible, Thompson pretended to be unconscious. "I can't describe it to you," he told reporter Stanley. "It just felt as if the whole head was taken right off. The Indian then mounted and galloped away, but as he went he dropped my scalp within a few feet of me, which I managed to get and hide. The Indians were thick in the vicinity, or I might then have made my escape. While lying down I could hear the Indians moving around whispering to each other, and then shortly after placing obstructions on the track. After lying down about an hour and a half I heard the low rumbling of the train as it came tearing along, and I might have been able to flag it off had I dared."

Thompson was not able to warn the approaching iron

William Thompson's scalp. *(Omaha Public Library)*

horse of the attack. The train plunged with several freight cars into the ditch, and the engineer and fireman were killed. The conductor and three other men in the caboose escaped and ran back down the track to warn a second freight train which was following close behind. William Thompson was able to escape while the Cheyennes were looting the cars.

Understandably, James Strobridge and the Central Pacific wanted to avoid such troubles with Indians that these other railroads had experienced. The problems the Union Pacific and the Kansas Pacific had on the Great Plains were warning enough. The Plum Creek ambush became a model to avoid. Strobridge decided to offer jobs to some of the native Americans, and he had the Central Pacific sign a special treaty with the Paiutes and Shoshones. "We gave the old chiefs a pass each, good on the passenger cars," Huntington said. "We told our men to let the Indians ride on the freight cars whenever they saw fit." Both male and female Indians worked easily alongside the Chinese. It was reported that the women could usually handle crowbars and sledgehammers better than the men.

On one occasion, the Paiutes accidentally caused a halt in the work on the grading of the Central Pacific between Reno and Wadsworth. They loved to tell tall tales and the Chinese who were working with them were a good audience. One tale they told the Orientals was about snakes in the Nevada desert so large they could swallow a man in one gulp. The story frightened the Chinese so much that five hundred of them started back that night to Sacramento. Charlie Crocker had to send several men out on horseback to round up the Chinese and tell them the Paiutes were joking about the large snakes.

On July 22, the tracks reached Wadsworth. Soon afterward, the first train from Sacramento rolled into the station. From there, the railroad would be built through the passes of the Humboldt Range. People who traveled overland to California dreaded this desert country. For five hundred miles it was a land of white alkali beds burned by the sun. It was waterless, treeless, and bare of vegetation except for gray sagebrush and little juniper trees. Timber for construction of tracks and for locomotive fuel had to be hauled from the Sierra forests. Special water trains carried huge wooden tanks of water on flatcars. The water filled the boilers of the iron horse as well as providing vital drinking water for the workmen.

Laying track through the Sierras had been so difficult and slow that Crocker and Strobridge now wanted to avoid building bridges and digging cuts because it took too much time and money. Instead, they built the railroad in snakeline curves. After all, each extra mile gave the Big Four twice the money it cost them to build. In a few years, millions more dollars would have to be spent to straighten those same hastily built tracks. They were laid so quickly and carelessly during the great race that miles and miles of them had to be rebuilt.

In September, after the tracklayers passed Mill City, a San Francisco reporter made the journey to the end of the track. He thought the names the Central Pacific had given its stations described the Nevada land very well. Desert, Hot Springs, Mirage, and Granite Point were some of the station names. He also noticed how careless the government was in its inspection and certification of the track. The reporter said that one inspector stood on the platform of the rear car and looked at the ties, rails, and grades through a spyglass as the train moved quickly along. As the man inspected, his assistant was taking a nap on the floor of the car. Their claim was "that if the passengers could sleep, the track must be level, easy, and all right; whereas if too rough to sleep, something must be wrong with the work."

The Central Pacific was building about a mile of new track a day, racing hard to beat the Union Pacific into Utah. As the Casement brothers of the Union Pacific had done, Strobridge put together a work train of a dozen cars. It had sleeping and dining areas, and shops for carpenters and telegraph-line builders. The first car was Strobridge's living quarters, and his wife kept it so neat that a newspaperman said her home on wheels was as nice as any home in San Francisco.

No matter how hard he drove his men, however, it looked as if the Union Pacific was going to reach Utah first. As the year of 1868 neared its end, it became apparent that the Union Pacific would have its tracks laid to the key city of Ogden before the Central Pacific got through the Promontory Range north of the Great Salt Lake. Brigham Young was displeased that both railroads had decided *not* to run their main tracks into Salt Lake City. Only a branch line from Ogden to Salt Lake City would be built. Young demanded control of the branch line, and he later operated this spur with train equipment he acquired from the Union Pacific. The equipment was partial payment for the work that the

Mormons had done as graders for the Union Pacific.

At the end of the year the Central Pacific's tracks neared Carlin, Nevada, 446 miles from Sacramento. The Union Pacific's rails reached Evanston, Wyoming, near the Utah border, 995 miles west of Omaha. Between the tracks less than 400 miles was left. Much of that area had already been graded for tracks running almost side by side. An air of excitement crossed America because it became apparent that the dream of a transcontinental railroad was coming true. When construction began the planners had hoped to finish the work in time for the nation's one hundredth birthday, the centennial celebration of 1876. Now it seemed possible that the two railroads would be joined in 1869, seven years early.

The rival railroads could easily have chosen a place where the two tracks would meet. But the railroad companies continued the wasteful construction of two parallel grades across Utah. Finally, the Union Pacific builders realized it would be foolish to continue grading west of Promontory toward Humboldt Wells in Nevada. After stopping at Promontory, they brought gangs of Irish graders into Utah to complete the tracks between that place and Ogden.

In the spring of 1869 each railroad company was grading a line of track between Ogden and Promontory. Grenville Dodge of the Union Pacific noticed that the Irish and the Chinese did not like each other, and he commented, "Our Irishmen were in the habit of firing their blasts in the cuts without giving warning to the Chinamen on the Central Pacific working right above them. From this cause several Chinamen were severely hurt. Complaint was made to me by the Central Pacific people, and I endeavored to have the contractors bring all hostilities to a close, but, for some reason or other they failed to do so. One day the Chinamen, appreciating the situation, put in what is called a 'grave' on their work, and when the Irishmen right under them were all at work, let go their blast and buried several of our men. This brought about a truce at once. From that time the Irish laborers showed due respect for the Chinamen, and there was no further trouble." Dodge may have exaggerated this story considerably, but it has become a part of the legend of the railroad.

The Union Pacific reached Ogden first but it cost them plenty of money, materials, and human lives. As in war, the longer the contest continued, the worse the leaders treated their men. The men in charge of the railroads really pushed their workmen hard. Deaths by accident were higher among the Central Pacific's Chinese workers; they lost between five hundred and a thousand. The Union Pacific lost more workmen from exposure to weather and diseases. Four Union Pacific workmen were murdered in the wild towns along the route for every one killed in an accident on the railroad itself. The railroad companies offered almost no medical help to the workmen.

In the spring of 1868, the Union Pacific came out of

General Jack Casement's construction train for the Union Pacific as it looked in 1868. The train carried everything from road building supplies and blacksmith shops to dining and sleeping cars for the workmen.

the long Wyoming winter to begin building track west of Cheyenne. Jack Casement's work train grew to be eighty cars long. It now included a bakery car, a bath car, a complete feed store and saddle shop, more kitchen, dining, and bunk cars, a combined telegraph and payroll car, and a butcher's car. The butcher's car was kept filled with fresh beef from a cattle herd that was driven each day next to the work train as it moved westward across Wyoming.

Sometimes a newspaper would set up shop for a short while in one of the cars. Stories would be written about events along the way. In case of Indian attacks, the Casements placed about a thousand rifles in racks in the ceilings of the cars. The railroad's good friend, General

Sherman, also ordered five thousand infantrymen and
cavalrymen to accompany the builders.

During April, a group of Union Pacific graders went
into Wyoming's Black Hills. They had to travel through
deep patches of snow to get there. A thousand tracklayers soon followed. On April 16, the iron rails reached
Sherman Summit, 8,242 feet above sea level. This was a
thousand feet higher than the Central Pacific's Summit
Tunnel in the Sierras. Grenville Dodge had surveyed
this pass to the Pacific Ocean in 1865 and named the
mountain peak "in honor of General Sherman, the
tallest general in the service." To celebrate reaching
Sherman Summit, Dr. Durant came out from New York
and personally placed the first rail. The Union Pacific

builders were very proud that they had reached the highest point that a railroad had reached anywhere in the world. Durant could not resist sending a boastful telegram to Leland Stanford of the Central Pacific. Stanford politely replied that his company was quite happy with reaching a peak of 7,017 feet themselves.

While the owners celebrated at Sherman Summit, bridge builders for the Union Pacific were nailing together the largest wooden bridge on the railroad. It was 650 feet long and 130 feet high and crossed Dale Creek. When winds blew up the canyon the bridge swayed dangerously. The government refused to approve the bridge until it was held with cables. The inspectors also insisted that Durant replace it within the year with a better, stronger bridge made of iron. "The highest railroad bridge in the world," the Union Pacific had bragged, but the men who first crossed it on an iron horse said they felt as if they were on a bridge of toothpicks.

The Union Pacific moved on to Laramie, a Wyoming town that was going through wild times. Attempts were made to enforce the law in Laramie and stop the violence there.

Another wild hell-on-wheels town was Benton, named for Senator Thomas Hart Benton. Water had to be hauled three miles by wagon from the North Platte River for a dollar a barrel, but Thomas Durant of the Union Pacific had no trouble selling lots to eager buyers. Two months later, Benton was a ghost town.

While Benton was at its busiest it had twenty-three saloons and five dance halls. Long freight trains arrived each day from the East to unload goods to be shipped by wagon westward. Newspaperman John Beadle described the mob of people that filled the streets for ten hours each day. "The streets were eight inches deep in white dust as I entered the city of canvas tents," he wrote, "and a new arrival with black clothes looked like nothing so much as a cockroach struggling through a flour barrel."

Before the city of Benton died, some of the tents were replaced with cheap buildings that had been shipped all the way from Chicago. These buildings were "prefabricated" and they appeared to be built of brick and brownstone. Actually they were merely boards painted to resemble these permanent materials.

Jack Casement, construction superintendent for the Union Pacific, wrote to his wife about Benton: "The meanest place I have ever been in." Casement especially hated the August heat. It slowed construction, and Utah was still miles away. Casement was also annoyed by the constant stream of visitors to the railroad. Thomas Durant invited these guests in the hopes that as members of special excursion parties on the railroad they would buy railroad stock. The most important excursion party of the summer was that of General Ulysses Grant. He was the candidate of the Republican party for President of the United States. As part of his campaign, Grant was traveling across the West, showing voters that he was as interested as everyone else in the transcontinental railroad.

As the summer came to an end, swarms of newspaper-men arrived daily from the East, to watch the great race between the two railroads. The newsmen sent bulletins back east "from the front" as though they were writing about a war. Each day's progress was reported. For example, one reporter wrote: "Sherman and his vic-torious legions sweeping from Atlanta to Savannah was a spectacle less glorious than this army of men marching on foot from Omaha to Sacramento, subduing unknown wildernesses, scaling unknown mountains, surmounting untried obstacles, and binding across the broad breast of America the iron emblem of modern progress and civilization."

Late in October, tracklayers were within a few miles of the Utah line. Each night ice rimmed the tops of the water barrels, warning them that winter would come early to the mountains. In November, they reached Bear River, in the heart of the old fur-trade country of Jim Bridger and the mountain men.

After they crossed into Utah, December snows made grading and tracklaying difficult for the men. Each day the foreman of the railroad gang expected to receive orders to stop work and make a winter camp. Despite the weather, work went on through the winter of 1868–69. The Central Pacific was moving rapidly across the desert, and because of the rival company's progress, Durant ordered the near-frozen men of the Union Pacific to move full speed ahead. Durant was still eager for more government money and land grants that would come to his company if they kept moving.

Now the workmen on the Union Pacific were suffering as the Central Pacific had suffered in the snows of the Sierras. They had to drag timber out of snowbanks and move dirt with picks and shovels. They laid track on icy crusts and blasted tunnels through the red sandstone of the canyons.

Grenville Dodge was as anxious as Durant was to beat the Central Pacific into Ogden, Utah. Dodge said, however, that laying the track in snow and ice might cost as much as over ten million dollars. It was difficult to work well on snow and ice because sometimes the trains slid off the track. Also if rails were laid down on snow and ice, which then melted, the ties and rails would be left dangling in the air. Long stretches of newly laid track were on such soft grade beds that the heavy trains would cause the track itself to slide off into the rivers below.

Accidents and deaths increased among the Union Pacific workers. When the men complained, the foremen reminded them that they were involved in a great race. Were the Irish tarriers of the Union Pacific going to let the Chinamen of the Central Pacific beat them into Ogden? Never! Jack Casement found plenty of track-layers still willing to work after sundown by lantern light in bitter cold. It seemed to be important to the Irishmen to prove that they could outwork the Chinese.

Christmas Day was celebrated in Wahsatch, where

the track was only sixty-seven miles from Ogden. Durant, in his private car was there for the celebration. Snow was piled high along the tracks. Newspaperman John Beadle reported that the temperature in the dining room of the town's only hotel was five degrees below zero. "A drop of the hottest coffee spilled upon the cloth froze in a minute, while the gravy was hard on the plate, and the butter froze in spite of the fastest eater."

The Union Pacific's worst blow of the winter came from the government. The Secretary of the Interior suddenly ordered the railroad to stop construction. Company headquarters was at Echo Summit, forty miles east of Ogden, when the order came to stop work. The railroad had already laid track several miles west of Echo Summit, and the graders were nearing Ogden. Despite the government orders to stop working, the Union Pacific boldly continued with construction.

On the morning of March 8, 1869, four days after Grant became President, Jack Casement's track gangs laid rails into Ogden. That afternoon an iron horse rolled in, its whistle drowning out the music of a welcoming brass band. Good news was received during the celebration. The new President, Ulysses Grant, had canceled the order (which the Union Pacific had ignored) to halt construction at Echo Summit.

As soon as the celebration ended, Casement started his tracklayers back to work. A month later they were at Corinne. This town would be the next to the last of the tent-and-tarpaper camps, the last of the hell-on-wheels towns that followed the railroad. A land agent for the Union Pacific named the town for his daughter (an act he must have later regretted). He called Corinne the "Chicago of the Rocky Mountains."

Only fifty miles now separated the railroads in the great race. It was obvious that they must meet somewhere in the Promontory Range. Yet no meeting place was chosen. Instead the railroads continued to build their grades past each other, often running side by side.

President Grant finally had to call for a meeting of the two companies. He wanted them to stop being so wasteful, and he let them know that if they could not decide where the tracks would join, the government would do it for them.

After an all-night meeting between Grenville Dodge of the Union Pacific and Collis Huntington of the Central Pacific, the location was chosen. The place for the joining of the two railroads would be Promontory Summit, Utah.

Promontory was to be the last of the railroad boom towns. It had one long street of tents and false-fronted wooden buildings, all set only a few yards back from the railroad tracks. After Promontory was chosen for the meeting of the rails, a special event was staged for newsmen and photographers who began arriving from East and West. For some time there had been rumors that Charlie Crocker of the Central Pacific had bet Thomas Durant of the Union Pacific that his workmen could lay ten miles of track in a single day. Durant did not believe that such a feat was possible. As the two railroads moved closer to Promontory, Crocker chose April 28 as the day to settle the bet.

For the railroad workmen, "Ten-Mile Day" was more important than the day of the final joining of the rails. Both companies announced that Ten-Mile Day would be a holiday except for the few men who would do the work. Crocker planned the action as if it were a military operation, ordering ties placed along the grade and bringing in carloads of rails, fishplates, bolts, and spikes. Chinese workmen on handcars pulled by horses moved the iron materials forward along the tracks.

A special crew of eight rail carriers was in charge of placing the rails. These eight iron men were the heroes of the day. Their names—Sullivan, Dailey, Kennedy, Joyce, Shaw, Eliott, Killeen, McNamara—tell us they probably came from Ireland.

Each workman moved rapidly, jumping, trotting, running and dancing as he worked. They rested very little, stopping only occasionally for a sip of water or tea. A special group of Chinese carried pails of refreshments to the tracklayers.

By one-thirty the men had laid six miles of rails and Crocker ordered a stop for lunch. He offered to let any tracklayer stop who had had enough. Nobody accepted the offer. An hour later they were back at work. At seven o'clock, James Strobridge made the sign for victory. In twelve hours, a full working day, the men had passed the ten-mile mark by fifty-six feet. During that

Marker boldly proclaiming ten miles of track were laid on a single
day.   (*Utah State Historical Society*)

day the tracklayers spiked 3,520 rails to 25,800 ties.
Each rail handler had lifted 250,000 pounds of iron.

Dr. Durant was not present to see the loss of his ten-
thousand-dollar bet to Charlie Crocker. But Grenville
Dodge was there. "I saw them lay their special ten miles
on that wager," he said. Dodge complained that the
men had spent a week preparing for the bet, by placing
the ties on the track.

Dodge was more interested in the joining of the rails
and the driving of the last spike. The special place
chosen to spike the last rail went by several names:

Promontory Point, Promontory Summit, Promontory Station, or just Promontory (after the railroad was finished). It lay in a waterless basin of sagebrush, ringed on three sides by mountains. Tracks of the Central Pacific reached Promontory on April 30. The California railroad had to wait a week before the Union Pacific tracklayers finally came into view. On May 1, hundreds of men lined up at the paymasters' cars of both railroads. The men were being paid their last wages. Seven thousand others had only one more week of work. "The two opposing armies," reported a newsman, "are melting away." The great race was coming to an end.

Driving the Golden Spike

On May 7, 1869, only 2,500 feet of empty grading lay between the two railroads. That afternoon, Leland Stanford's special train arrived for the celebration that was planned for May 8. But Jack Casement of the Union Pacific told the Central Pacific's president that there would be a delay in their plans. Casement said that heavy rains had washed out part of his tracks and that the special train carrying Thomas Durant and other officials could not move. They would have to repair the track and the celebration would have to be postponed until May 10.

But there was more to the story than that. On May 6, the special Union Pacific train had pulled into Piedmont, Wyoming, from the East. When it stopped, an armed mob of several hundred railroad workers surrounded Durant's private car. They moved it onto a sidetrack and chained the wheels to the rails. Spokes-

men for the workers told the startled Dr. Durant that
they wanted their overdue wages. Durant and his important associates would be kept prisoners until the
workmen were paid.

How much the workmen asked for and received is
unknown. Union Pacific officials tried to keep it a secret.
It may have been twelve thousand dollars, but it may
have been as much as two hundred and thirty-five thousand dollars. Some historians think the Mormons were
the leaders of the angry mob because Brigham Young
had not been paid all that the railroad had promised
him. Durant tried to obtain the help of soldiers from
nearby Army posts, but telegrams to the military were
stopped by the angry workers. Durant finally gave up
and sent to New York for payroll funds.

A cold rain fell on Sunday, May 9, but the railroads
were ready for the final tracklaying. The next morning
the weather cleared into a perfect day for the celebration. White clouds floated on a clean blue sky against a
distant backdrop of cedar-covered mountains. A cool
breeze blew and the temperature rose to sixty-nine
degrees.

By seven o'clock the first curious onlookers had arrived. They gathered around the small gap in the track
which the two railroads would close that day. The nation's first transcontinental railroad was only two rails
away from being completed. A huge American flag
flapped from a nearby telegraph pole, and next to the
tracks, peddlers had already set up tents to sell whiskey.

At about eight o'clock a construction train arrived and out jumped the lively tracklayers and graders. The train then backed down the track.

Shortly after ten o'clock, two Union Pacific trains pulled up and stopped a short distance from the gap in the tracks. The first train was Durant's delayed three-car special. Riding with him were Dodge, Seymour, Reed, the Casement brothers, and several other officials and guests. Aboard the second train were five companies of the 21st U. S. Infantry and its band. Another group included important Utah citizens and a brass band from Salt Lake City.

While these arrivals were getting off the train, a gang of Chinese dressed in blue began smoothing out the gap in the roadbed. They laid the last ties and rails and bolted on the fishplates. They drove all but the last few spikes. At eleven-fifteen the Central Pacific train puffed into view. Both iron horses were uncoupled and brought down their tracks. The Central Pacific's locomotive was called Jupiter and had a flared funnel stack. The Union Pacific's No. 119 had a straight stack with a spark-arrester on top. The locomotives stood facing each other across the meeting place of the rails. The soldiers of the 21st U.S. Infantry formed a double line facing the tracks and stood at parade rest.

By this time Stanford and the members of his party were shaking hands with the officials of the Union Pacific. They began discussing the plans for the ceremonies. Stanford had brought along two golden spikes, a silver spike, a combination spike of iron and silver and gold, a silver-plated sledgehammer, and a polished laurel tie.

Although Stanford had assembled all these ceremonial symbols, very little planning had been done about the actual proceedings for the joining of the rails. They began to disagree about the program. Dr. Durant, dressed in a stylish black velvet jacket, was suffering from a bad headache. This was probably caused by all the champagne he had drunk the day before, and he wanted to hurry through the spike ceremony. Grenville Dodge did not like Stanford's fancy spikes and hammers and wanted to drive the last spike himself, using a plain iron spike.

Even to the very last hour, the officials of the two railroads in the great race had trouble agreeing with each other. It was now eleven fifty-five, only five minutes before the chosen time for the joining of the rails. Durant made the final decision to use Stanford's plan to drive a golden spike.

Nobody present that day could remember how large the crowd was, although the estimated number ranged from five hundred to three thousand. Photographs taken of the event indicate that there were six or seven hundred people present. Among them were the companies of the 21st U. S. Infantry and about twenty reporters and photographers. Twenty women also were present, most of whom were wives of railroad officials and Army officers. "It was not a large crowd," Sidney Dillon, a

Union Pacific official, later recalled. He added that the ground-breaking ceremony at Omaha had been much livelier, with more brass bands, fireworks, and speeches. That had been less than five years earlier.

An explanation for the small crowd at Promontory was that in 1869 that remote part of Utah was difficult to reach. Yet it can be said that the *spirit* of America was truly there for the joining of the rails. Americans across the country eagerly waited for telegraph flashes to signal the great event.

To speed up the messages, a wire had been run from a telegraph pole to a key on a small table facing the gap between the rails. At twelve-twenty, W. N. Shilling, Western Union's telegraph operator, tapped out a message. He announced that in about twenty minutes the last spike would be driven. Operators across the nation quickly cleared their lines. While Shilling's key chattered, James Strobridge and Sam Reed brought up the laurel tie into which spike holes had already been driven. The eager onlookers now pushed so close that Jack Casement had to order them back, so that photographers and their cameras could move forward to record the event.

Durant stepped forward to accept the two gold spikes from a representative of the Central Pacific. He kneeled and slid them into the prepared holes in the laurel tie, his eyes blinking at the inscribed silver plate: THE LAST TIE LAID ON THE COMPLETION OF THE PACIFIC RAILROAD, MAY 1869. As he arose, Leland Stanford began speaking in the bright sunlight, his voice strong at the end: "Now, gentlemen, with your assistance we will proceed to lay the last tie, the last rail, and drive the last spike."

While the crowd cheered and the bands played, the other spikes and the silver-plated sledgehammer were brought forward. After a telegraph wire was attached to the last spike, Stanford raised the sledgehammer and brought it down briskly, missing the spike entirely. The watching tracklayers roared with laughter. Durant put on a pair of gloves to protect his tender palms, lifted the sledgehammer, and also missed. Aware that the blows of the sledgehammer had not gone out over the wire, telegrapher Shilling touched his key and tapped out: "Done." James Strobridge and Samuel Reed stepped forward and took turns driving down the spike. The time was twelve forty-seven. "We all yelled like to bust," was the way one of the spectators described it.

After the gold and silver spikes and the laurel tie were carefully removed and replaced with an ordinary tie and iron spikes, the Central Pacific's Jupiter and the Union Pacific's No. 119 eased forward until their pilots clanged together. While cheering workmen climbed up onto both iron horses, their engineers scrambled to the boiler fronts with bottles of champagne, to shake hands and exchange toasts. The photographers worked frantically to clear the crowd back so that the railroad's chief engineers, Grenville Dodge and Samuel Montague, could stand before the two locomotives in another symbolic handclasp.

Moments before the last rail was laid at Promontory. Telegrapher's table is at right center.

*(Photo by A. J. Russell, Courtesy of
The Oakland Museum History Department)*

As soon as the wet-plate photographs were made, the Jupiter reversed its wheels and made room for No. 119 to cross the rail junction. Then No. 119 backed up, and the Jupiter with a merry whistle blast eased across to the Union Pacific's tracks. The transcontinental railroad was ready for the iron horses to roll.

7:

First Travelers
on the Transcontinental

On May 15, 1869, regular service began for travelers on America's first transcontinental railroad. Thousands of Americans who had become accustomed to train travel in the Eastern states could now journey behind an iron horse all the way to the Pacific Ocean. Most train trips across the continent included transfers in Chicago and Omaha, and in Promontory or Ogden. It was only in special cases that someone could board a car in an Eastern city and travel to California without a single transfer. The pioneer train travelers usually enjoyed transfer stops as welcome breaks in an eight- or ten-day adventure.

"Every man who could command the time and money was eager to make the trip," declared that energetic traveling reporter John Beadle, "and everybody who could sling ink became correspondents." From the beginning, many travelers did indeed write about their experiences on the railroad.

During the first year of transcontinental service, passengers from the East arrived in Chicago on the Michigan Central Railroad. By the mid-1870s, travelers had the choice of riding the Pennsylvania, Erie, or New York Central.

"Seventy-five minutes are allowed for getting from the station of arrival to the station of departure," said William F. Rae, an Englishman who made the journey late in 1869. "In my own case the times of the trains did not correspond; the one train had started an hour before the other arrived." Because he had planned to stop over for a short while in Chicago, Rae was not disappointed in the delay of twenty-four hours, but many of his fellow passengers were. For another century, travelers passing through Chicago would continue to have problems with changing trains and missing connections. During the heyday of American passenger travel, one of the common sayings was that a hog could travel across country through Chicago without changing cars. A human being could not.

To make connections with the Union Pacific from Chicago, travelers had a choice of two direct routes, the Rock Island or the Northwestern, and an indirect route, the Chicago, Burlington & Quincy. People who knew about the direct routes soon learned to avoid the evening express trains. These trains would leave passengers stranded in Council Bluffs or Omaha, sometimes for twenty-four hours.

Until a bridge was completed in 1871, it was necessary for Western travelers to cross the Missouri River "in a rickety old ferryboat" from Council Bluffs to Omaha. "On arriving at Council Bluffs," reported William Rae, "we found omnibuses in waiting at the station. The morning was cold and raw. But a small proportion of the passengers could get inside seats, the remainder having the option of either sitting on the roof among the luggage, or else being left behind . . . Through deep ruts in the mud the omnibus was slowly drawn by four horses to the river's bank, and thence on to the deck of a flat-bottomed steamer."

After a bridge was built across the Missouri, the railroads refused to take the cars of the Eastern roads across "Big Muddy" to the Union Pacific station. When passengers arrived in Council Bluffs, they had to move themselves and their luggage to the cars of the Transfer Company, "whose province is to put passengers to all sort of inconvenience and trouble in crossing over the river." John Erastus Lester of Providence, Rhode Island, traveled west in 1872 in the hope of improving his health. He described the passage by the Transfer Company as having "caused more hard words to be spoken than can be erased from the *big book* for many a day." Lester was one of many people who disliked the company's treatment of passengers. Also, the task of unloading freight from Eastern cars and repacking it for shipment across the river was troublesome.

Early travelers on the transcontinental railroad saw little to admire in Omaha. One person called it "the muddiest place I ever saw," but added that "the roads

At arrival and departure times, the Omaha station was a scene of
bustling confusion.   *(Nebraska State Historical Society)*

are generally deep with dust." Another described the
town as being layered with mud through which "the
omnibus labored slowly, the outside passengers being
advised by the driver to move about from one side of
the roof to another, in order to guard against upsetting
the overloaded vehicle. A general feeling of relief was
manifested when the station of the Union Pacific was
reached."

Almost all passengers agreed that the Omaha station
was very noisy and full of confusion, especially at the
times of train departure. The journey to the West was
considered to be a daring activity during these early
years. Rumors were spread among the ticket buyers of
the possibility that Indians would attack or wreck the

trains. In Omaha, these rumors aided railroad agents in the sale of insurance policies for the people traveling west.

Except for a quick whistle from the engine and the conductor's cry of "All aboard!" there was no warning of the train's departure from the Omaha station. This usually resulted in a rush of passengers who had to hop on board the already moving cars.

John Lester recorded the scenery outside of Omaha: "For three or four miles we pass along the bluffs . . . and then push out upon the open prairie, the fertile lands of Nebraska. A vast plain, dotted here and there with trees, stretches away upon every side."

In the springtime, the rolling land was covered with wild flowers. Their fragrance drifted into the open windows of cars moving along at twenty miles an hour. In summer, tumbleweeds by the thousands wheeled across the drying grass. By autumn, prairie fires blazed against the horizon. William Rae wrote about the "spectacle of a prairie fire," saying that "for miles on every side the air is heavy with volumes of stifling smoke, and the ground reddened with hissing and rushing fire."

Travelers from other countries found the Great Plains grass shorter than they had expected. The grass was often compared to a sweep of grayish-green ocean waves. Some travelers complained of their eyes becoming tired because of the sameness of the landscape. They said the train seemed at times to be standing still in a huge field of grass. All travelers welcomed the first break in the Plains landscape, which was the ribbon of the Platte River. The railroad followed this river westward, just as the wagon trains of earlier years had followed it.

When the transcontinental railroad opened for service, George Mortimer Pullman had been building experimental sleeping cars for four years. In 1869 the Union Pacific bought several of these cars, which were called Pullman Palace cars. They were painted in rich brown colors, quite different from the ordinary drab coach cars. Every traveler who could afford the price would pay the extra twenty-five dollars for first-class fare and four dollars a day for a Pullman Palace car. They were eager for the comfort of sleeping in a berth. First-class travelers paid one hundred dollars for the journey from Omaha to Sacramento. Second-class or coach cost seventy-five dollars. There was also a special rate of forty dollars for immigrants, who rode cramped together on uncomfortable board seats. The express trip usually lasted four to five days; by mixed train, the trip was six to seven days, including transfers. The speed of the trains varied according to the condition of the tracks and bridges. Rough and carelessly built tracks slowed the trains down to nine miles per hour. The speed increased to thirty-five miles per hour over smoother tracks. Most travelers of the early 1870s mentioned in their journals that speeds of eighteen to twenty-two miles per hour were average. Although speeds were doubled over the next ten years, the stops and starts at more than two hundred stations and water tanks were time-consuming. These delays consequently prevented the long journey from being shortened.

Even in an era when the most highly skilled Americans earned less than a hundred dollars a month, there was great demand for hundred-dollar Pullman space on the transcontinental railroad. Early in the 1870s, the Union Pacific began running three sleeping cars on some trains and still had to turn away would-be ticket buyers. Because George Pullman was interested in the Union Pacific, he supplied that railroad with special luxuries. Travelers heard or read about the Palace cars on the Union Pacific and were eager to ride on them no matter what they cost. "I had a sofa to myself, with a table and a lamp," wrote a happy rider. "The sofas are widened and made into beds at night. My berth was three feet three inches wide, and six feet three inches long. It had two windows looking out of the train, a handsome mirror, and was well furnished with bedding and curtains."

British travelers were especially impressed with the Pullman Palace cars. Some of them sent letters to railway directors in London, writing that they hoped British companies would copy the American trains, ". . . and provide sleeping carriages for long night journeys." The British also enjoyed the freedom of moving from one car to another. One traveler, however, who signed himself "A London Parson," admitted that trying to dress himself in a box two feet high was a bit difficult. "It was an odd experience, that going to bed of some

Westbound travelers were eager to ride on the deluxe Pullman Palace cars no matter what the cost. *(Picture Collection, The Branch Libraries, The New York Public Library)*

thirty ladies, gentlemen, and children, in, practically, one room. For two nights I had a young married couple sleeping in the berth above mine. The lady turned in first, and presently her gown was hung out over the rail to which her bed curtains were fastened. But further processes of unrobing were indicated by the agitation of the drapery which concealed her nest. As the same curtain served for both berths—hers and mine—the gentle-

In cold weather, passengers scrambled for a place at the foot warmer. *(Culver Pictures, Inc.)*

man held her portion together over my head when it was necessary for me to retire. At last all were housed, and some snores rose above the rattle of the train. I did not sleep much the first night, but looked over the moonlit prairie from my pillow."

Mr. Pullman introduced a "hotel car" in 1870 with a kitchen at one end. Meals were served on removable tables set between the drawing-room seats. This was convenient, but at first the Union Pacific only scheduled the special "hotel car" for one trip each week. Until well into the 1880s it was usual for the transcontinental railroads to have their passengers dine at stations along the route. The passengers were allowed only about thirty minutes at the dining stations to bolt down their meals before continuing on the journey.

Comments on the meals at the dining stops were often not favorable. The first stop out of Omaha was Grand Island, and one passenger commented that the food there was "ill cooked and poorly served." William Robertson of Scotland said bluntly, "We found the quality on the whole bad . . . and all three meals, breakfast, dinner and supper, were almost identical, viz., tea, buffalo steaks, antelope chops, sweet potatoes, and boiled Indian corn, with hoe cakes and syrup ad nauseam." Susan Coolidge from New York also complained about the boring diet: "It was necessary to look at one's watch to tell whether it was breakfast, dinner or supper that we were eating, these meals presenting invariably the same salient features of beefsteak, fried eggs, fried potato." Miss Coolidge was generous enough to compliment the chef of Sidney, Nebraska, for serving ". . . cubes of fried mush . . . of unusual excellence."

Harvey Rice of Cleveland, Ohio, described the Sidney breakfast station as a crude building constructed of boards and canvas. He said the passengers were fed what they thought was an excellent breakfast of chicken stew, ". . . but which, they were afterward informed, consisted of prairie dogs—a new variety of chickens, without feathers. This information created an unpleasant sensation in sundry delicate stomachs."

According to William L. Humason of Hartford, Connecticut, the farther a person traveled west across the plains, the worse the dining stations became, ". . . consisting of miserable shanties, with tables dirty, and waiters not only dirty, but saucy. The tea tasted as though it were made from the leaves of the sagebrush—literally *sage tea*. The biscuit was made without soda, but with plenty of alkali, harmonizing with the great quantity of alkali dust we had already swallowed." The only dining station Humason had a good word for was at Cisco, California, where he said the water on the table was as clear as crystal. He thought, however, that a dollar and a quarter was ". . . a pretty steep price to pay for fried ham and potatoes."

At most dining stops, however, meal prices were one dollar. On the California section of the Central Pacific the prices were reduced to seventy-five cents if the diner paid in silver rather than in paper money. Neither the Union Pacific nor the Central Pacific ran their own eating houses. They had contracts with private individuals and the quality of the service varied greatly. The eating houses were usually located in rough wooden buildings, where large platters of food would be waiting for the passengers when they came down from the trains.

Eventually, some of the stations grew to have reputations for special foods. There was good beefsteak at

Laramie, delicious hot biscuits at Green River, antelope at Sidney, and fish at Colfax. The favorite stop was at Evanston, Wyoming, where mountain trout was the specialty. "It was kept by a colored man named Howard W. Crossley whose evident desire was to please all," wrote John Lester.

Because Cheyenne was listed in the guidebooks as the largest city between Omaha and Sacramento, many passengers expected to find excellent food there. Actually, Cheyenne was a small town full of board and canvas buildings and three thousand miners in big boots. "The chops were generally as tough as hanks of whipcord, and the knives as blunt as bricklayers' trowels," said a passenger of the dining station. Some people thought the antelope steaks in Cheyenne were tasty, but Susan Coolidge did not like them. She suggested that whenever beefsteak was too tough, the dining stations called it "antelope" to give it the charm of being something special.

Before her journey ended she decided that transcontinental travelers should pack a lunch basket consisting of Albert biscuit, orange marmalade, fresh rolls, and cold roasted chicken, which could be obtained at Omaha and Ogden.

Besides stops for meals, passengers passed the time by watching wildlife through the windows of the train. Unfamiliar animals such as antelope and prairie dogs could be seen alongside the track. Long files of fleet-footed antelope often came very close to the passing

Cheyenne's railroad dining room. *(Photo by A. J. Russell,*
Courtesy of The Oakland Museum History Department)

trains, seeming to be ". . . racing with the cars, and always winning in the race." Sometimes hunters fired upon these animals with rifles and pistols from the open windows of the cars. The Union Pacific Railroad did not approve of the activity, but few hits were recorded anyway.

Villages of prairie dogs were close enough to the railroad for passengers to watch the friendly rodents sitting at the doors of their burrows. "They fling themselves in the air with a gay nimbleness beautiful to see, flip a somersault, and present to the admiring gaze of the traveler two heels and a short furry tail as they make their exit from the stage of action."

Elk, wolves, and bears were also often spotted as the iron horse thundered across the West. One traveler was sure that he saw a pack of wild dogs trotting along next to the railroad, until he learned they were coyotes. Another unfamiliar sight was swarms of grasshoppers and crickets. Sometimes masses of these insects settled on the tracks, causing the locomotive wheels to spin into a temporary stall.

After train travel began, only thinning herds of buffalo remained near the Union Pacific tracks. Less than two hundred miles to the south, however, the iron horses of the Kansas Pacific were often surrounded by buffalo. Sometimes they had to slow down until the herd passed. One traveler on that railroad told of seeing a herd that reached as far as the eye could reach. "With heads down and tails up they galloped towards the track making extraordinary exertions to get across ahead of the locomotive. In trying this strategic feat one specimen found himself forcibly lifted into the air and thrown into the ditch, where he lay upon his back, his cloven feet flourishing madly."

The buffalo and other animals entertained the travelers against a constantly changing background of scenery. The landscape became more and more fascinating the farther they traveled from the Plains. The first glimpse of the snow range of the Rocky Mountains always sent a wave of excitement through the passenger cars. "My boyish dreams were realized," one man recorded. "For hours, at the school desk, have I pondered over the map and wandered, in my imagination, with Lewis and Clark, the hunters and trappers and early emigrants, away off to those Rocky Mountains, about which such a mystery seemed to hang—dreaming, wishing and hoping against hope, that my eyes might, some day, behold their snow-crowned heights. And here lay the first range in the pureness of white; distant, to be sure, but there it lay, enshrined in beauty."

Wyoming was filled with wonders for these Eastern travelers. When the iron horse brought them through tunnels into Utah's Echo and Weber canyons, they found it difficult to find words to describe the towering castlelike rocks. "Grand beyond description . . . castles in the air . . . fantastic shapes and profiles . . . the scene is as fearful as it is sublime." Shortly after entering the narrows of Weber Canyon, almost every traveler who

kept a diary noted the Thousand-Mile Tree. This single
green pine, standing alone in rock and sage, marked the
distance of one thousand miles from Omaha. European
travelers compared Weber Canyon to canyons in the
European Alps. Castle Rock, Hanging Rock, Pulpit
Rock, Devil's Gate, and Devil's Slide were some of the
names scribbled into the notebooks of travelers. Many
of them seemed to think these rock formations were the
creations of God or Satan.

When there were no unusual animals or scenery to
look at, the passengers found other things to think
about. The ever-changing weather of the West was interesting. The train on which Harvey Rice was riding to
California in 1869 ran through a typically violent Great
Plains thunderstorm. "The heavens became, suddenly,
as black as starless midnight. The lightning flashed in
every direction, and electric balls of fire rolled over the
plains. It seemed as if the artillery of heaven had made
the valley a target and that we were doomed to instant
destruction. But happily our fears were soon dissipated.
The storm was succeeded by a brilliant rainbow."

Travel in winter would often include magnificent
snowstorms or fierce blizzards. Travelers could expect
the weather to make a transcontinental trip very difficult. On William Rae's return trip east from California
in the winter of 1870, he ran into a blizzard. The iron
horse pulling his train was forced into a two-hour battle
with the storm across the Laramie plains. Delays were
caused by the thick snow on the single-track Union

Pacific, but the passengers kept warm. Rae reported that the hot-air stove in his Pullman car made it "as comfortable as the best-warmed room in an English house."

Almost every pioneer rider on the transcontinental wanted to see a "real wild Indian." Few of them did, because the true Indian warriors of the Plains hated the iron horse and stayed far away from it. Even the tribes still at war with the United States had finally realized that they could not stop the iron tracks of the Union Pacific from being built. Indian leaders signed treaties that removed their people from the large areas of land taken by the railroad. Buffalo herds, also, fled far to the north and south of the path of the iron horse. Therefore, the Indians that the train travelers spotted on their journeys were usually those who had given up their Indian ways.

A few members of the Mississippi Valley Indian tribes were seen in railroad stations from Chicago to Omaha. These Indians still braided their hair, but they wore white men's clothing and had taken on many other white men's customs. The westbound travelers' first glimpse of the Plains Indians was usually around the Loup Fork in Nebraska, where the Pawnees lived on a reservation. Although the Pawnees had given up much of their horse-buffalo culture, the warriors still shaved their heads to a tuft of hair on top. They painted their faces and wore feathers and blankets. To travelers fresh from the East, the Pawnees had a very bloodthirsty appearance. Some guidebooks claimed that every one of them had scalps waving from the tops of lodgepoles.

Anywhere across western Nebraska or Wyoming, a traveler might catch a quick glimpse of a passing Sioux, Cheyenne, Arapaho, or Crow. These Indians staring at the passing iron horses were few and far between, however. By the time the train reached Nevada there were large groups of Shoshones and Paiutes grouped around nearly every station. These Indians frequently used treaty rights with the Central Pacific to ride the cars back and forth on the railroad. Because they lived in the desert, they were often covered with dust, and for lack of water they were often unbathed. As the passengers were offended by their dust and dirt, the Central Pacific made special rules for their train-riding. At first, the Indians were allowed only in the emigrants' coaches. After the emigrants complained of their presence, they had to ride in the baggage cars or outside on the boarding steps.

"We were regaled with the sight, for the first time, of a group of wild Indians," a traveler noted at one of the Nevada stations. "Some of the squaws were burdened with papooses strapped to their backs. They expected and received a 'shower' of donations from the passengers . . . This made them happy." The Indian women soon discovered how eager the travelers on the trains were to see their infants snuggled in basket cradles. They would ask for ten cents to a quarter in exchange for a look inside.

Lady Duffus Hardy was more interested in the male Indians who were loading wood into the locomotive tender. "The men stood in groups, solemnly regarding us with their big black eyes, still as statues; the women squatted on the platform or peeped at us from round corners. It was not exactly pleasant, but very interesting to find ourselves amid a score or two of this savage race, the men all armed with guns and knives."

Other travelers spent time worrying about what the warlike Indians might do if they were to put their minds to it. "It would be an easy matter," wrote an uneasy man from New England, "for them to rush on to an unprotected portion of the road, in the night, tear up the track, withdraw until the train comes up, is thrown from the track, or brought to a standstill, then rush forward again, and tear up the track in the rear of the cars, and thus have all the passengers at their mercy." After thinking over these possibilities, he added: "The poor Indian has few friends, and his days will soon be numbered."

These uneasy passengers might have spent their time better if they had worried about train robbers of the white race. Jesse James, for example, was far more likely to wreck and rob a train in the 1870s than were the Indians. Only eighteen months after the rails were joined at Promontory, a gang of six robbers quietly boarded the eastbound Central Pacific express at Truckee, California. An hour later, at one-thirty in the morning on November 4, 1870, the train stopped at

Verdi, Nevada, for fuel and water. Just as the engineer got his locomotive rolling again, one of the robbers dropped down from the tender into the cab of the engine. He pointed a pair of pistols at the engineer and fireman and ordered them to stop the train. The man's five companions jumped from the first coach and unfastened it from the express car. A few seconds later, the engineer and express car with six robbers aboard were moving rapidly away in the darkness.

Taking the express agent by surprise, the robbers broke in and stole the entire Virginia City payroll of more than forty thousand dollars. When the robbers left the express car, the engineer backed his shortened train nine miles back to Verdi. Here a bewildered conductor waited for him with several cars of sleeping passengers. Few of the travelers were aware of the robbery. Although this was the first robbery on the Central Pacific, the same act was repeated only twenty-four hours later on the same train. The second haul was four hundred miles farther east, near Toano, Nevada. The amount taken was almost as large as the first. After these robberies, Wells, Fargo hired armed guards to travel with valuable train shipments. Nevertheless, holdups continued for many years on the Central Pacific. The railroad that replaced the Central Pacific in later years, the Southern Pacific, also suffered from robberies.

The Union Pacific seemed to keep a tighter security on its express shipments. The first robbery on that line did not occur until August 27, 1875, near Bitter Creek,

Wyoming. Two bandits entered a moving express car through an unbarred window. They found the express agent asleep. Instead of jumping him and tying him up, they made the mistake of trying to get his keys out of his pocket. This woke him up, of course, and in the melee that followed, several wild shots were fired. The expressman pulled the bell cord to signal the engineer to stop the train. The robbers quickly grabbed armloads of packages and fled. They were not captured, but all they gained for their efforts were a few articles of little value.

Three years later, Big Nose George Parrot and Dutch Charlie Burris decided to derail a Union Pacific payroll train near Rawlins, Wyoming. They loosened a rail on a curve and waited hopefully in a nearby willow thicket for the train to come along. As luck would have it, that afternoon a railroad section boss made a walking inspection of the track. The spikes that Parrot and Burris had removed lay beside the loose rail. The section boss looked at the missing spikes and knew instantly that would-be robbers were probably hiding nearby. He pretended not to notice the spikes and walked on. When he was out of sight and around the curve, he ran as fast as he could, saw the approaching train, and flagged it to a stop. He learned afterward that the hidden robbers had their rifles aimed at him. Big Nose George had almost put a bullet in his back, but decided the track walker had not seen the missing rail and didn't shoot.

A posse was soon formed and went off to chase the robbers. Parrot and Burris killed two of the deputies,

Train robbery on the Union Pacific.   *(Culver Pictures, Inc.)*

and escaped to Montana. Several months passed before they were captured. While they were being returned to Rawlins for trial, an angry mob invaded the train they were riding. Before the sheriff and his men could stop them, the mob had grabbed Dutch Charlie Burris and hanged him from a telegraph pole. The sheriff managed to get Big Nose George into jail. Rumors spread that he tried to escape, and another gang of men broke into the jail and hanged him also.

The most-feared robber was Jesse James. The very

first train he robbed carried a load of transcontinental travelers on the Rock Island line between Adair and Council Bluffs. The James boys loosened a rail and tied a rope to it. When the train came rumbling into view, they jerked the rail off the track. The locomotive fell to its side, killing the engineer and injuring a number of passengers. Some of the gang of outlaws entered the express car and others marched through the coaches, robbing the surprised travelers of their money, watches, and jewelry. Jesse James and his group were on their horses riding for the Missouri hills before the train crew or passengers fully realized what had happened.

Not every train wreck was the result of a robbery. Because trains moved slowly in the early years, passengers were more often bruised than killed, unless the accident happened on a high bridge or mountain shoulder. Poor tracks and hot boxes (overheating of axle bearings) caused many accidents. A surprising number of passengers were injured from falling or jumping out of open windows. One of the pioneer passengers of 1869 wrote about the experience of a wreck in Echo Canyon. "On we bounded over the ties, the car wheels breaking many of them as though they were but pipe-stems. Every instant we expected to roll down the ravine. We ordered the ladies to cling to the sides of the seats and keep their feet clear of the floor. It seemed as if that train could never be stopped! But it was brought to a standstill upon the brink of an embankment. Had the cars gone a few rods further the reader would probably never have been troubled by these hastily written pages."

Another westbound traveler during that first year told of being shaken out of his seat on the Central Pacific. The train ran into a herd of cattle between Wadsworth and Clark's Station, Nevada, and the collision threw the locomotive off the track. A telegrapher aboard climbed the nearest pole and tapped the line, calling another engine to the rescue. There was an eight-hour delay, but the passengers made the best of their time. So as not to go hungry, they butchered the dead cattle, built a fire, and cooked steaks. Such accidents with cattle were among the most common causes of wrecks in the West. Railroad men and ranchers had many disagreements for more than half a century over the rights of cattle to be herded on railroad property.

Within a few weeks after the transcontinental railroad began running, a large number of guidebooks for travelers appeared for sale. The main railroad terminals offered the most popular guidebooks, including Crofutt's, Appleton's and Williams'. H. Wallace Atwell, who signed himself "Bill Dadd, the Scribe," led the Crofutt guides with his *Great Transcontinental Railroad Guide.* Mr. Crofutt claimed that he sold half a million copies of his guides during the 1870s.

Even people who never left their homes in the East read these guidebooks. And thanks to several excellent photographers and the "magic lantern" it was possible to enjoy the thrills of Western railroad travel without actually making the journey. The magic lantern, invented in the 1860s, contained a lamp that burned gas and calcium. Through a lens opening it projected brilliant limelight pictures upon a screen. For the first time, large audiences could view magnified images of photographs.

Stephen James Sedgwick, a former New York schoolteacher, earned a handsome income during the 1870s by taking audiences in Manhattan, Queens, Long Island, Connecticut, and New Jersey on magic lantern tours of the new transcontinental railroad. His collection of photographs of awe-inspiring scenes along the railroad no doubt inspired many in his audiences to undertake the real journey west.

Some of the railroad guidebooks offered more fiction than fact for the reader, but almost all included useful down-to-earth advice. Women, especially, did not always know what to take with them on the long journey across the nation. In addition to the usual baggage, the guides sometimes suggested that a woman bring a variety of items, such as: nightdress, clean collars and cuffs, pocket handkerchiefs and stockings, a bottle of cologne, a vial of powdered borax to soften the Western water, a warm flannel sack for sleeping on chilly nights, a whisk broom. Also suggested were a pocket pin cushion, a brandy flask, and two linen dusters. On leaving Omaha, another guide recommended, a lady should wear a light spring suit; and on the second day as the train approached the Rockies, a change to a winter suit was suggested. On the third day across Utah and the Nevada desert, she should wear a summer suit. On the fourth day in the Sierras, the winter suit and "all your underclothing" would be required. The fifth and last day would of course bring her into sunny California and the summer suit again.

Bill Dadd, the Scribe, was not very polite toward women travelers: "It is not right or just for a *lady* to occupy one whole seat with her flounces and herself, and another with her satchel, parasol, big box, little box, bandbox and bundle, as we have often seen them do, while plain-dressed, hard-handed toiling men are obliged to remain standing in the crowded car. The woman who indulges in such flights of fancy as to suppose that one fare entitles her to monopolize three seats should not travel until bloomers come in fashion."

In *The Pacific Tourist,* Henry Williams suggested that sometimes on the journey, a person should "sit and read, play games, and indulge in social conversation and glee." This guidebook author probably was referring to plays and musical events improvised by the Pullman passengers. In the early 1870s some Pullman cars had organs installed in them, and amateur musicians and professional traveling troupes of musicians often performed together. "Music sounds upon the prairie and dies away far over the plains; merry-making and jokes, conversation and reading pass the time pleasantly until ten o'clock, when we retire . . . If people who are traveling together will only try to make those about them happy, then a good time is assured. The second night on the road we arranged a little entertainment in the car and invited the ladies and gentlemen from the other cars into our 'improvised Music Hall.' The exercises consisted principally of recitations . . . The young ladies sang for us; and we were all happy—for the time at least."

The custom on Sundays was to hold religious services in one of the cars. On a train rolling through western Wyoming in 1872, John Lester read the Episcopal service and the Reverend Mr. Murray gave a sermon called "To Die is to Gain . . ." A choir sang "Nearer, My God, to Thee" and the national anthem. "Here in the very midst of the Rocky Mountain Wilderness," wrote Lester, "our thanksgivings were offered up; and our music floated out upon the air, and resounded through the deep caverns, and among the towering hills."

Among the most popular activities for passing the time were cardplaying, talking, and reading. "We had an abundant supply of books and newspapers," a surprised Englishman noted. "A boy frequently traversed the train with a good store of novels, mostly English, periodicals, etc." In the evening the travelers would often play whist, euchre, poker, or some other card game.

As in any era, travelers found plenty of entertainment by watching their fellow passengers. "It was curious to see a rough-booted, broad-brimmed fellow strutting up and down the train with his revolver slung behind him like a short blunt tail," said the London parson. "But, of course, if you leave them alone they don't meddle with you. They only shoot their friends and acquaintances, as a rule." Travelers from other countries disliked the widespread American habit of chewing tobacco. Many coaches and Pullmans provided special containers, called cuspidors, for tobacco-chewers to spit into. By the time they had crossed the American continent, foreign travelers had grown accustomed to seeing their fellow passengers spewing fountains of tobacco juice into the cuspidors. They also got used to sharing their seats with burly miners who boarded the trains with pockets full of tobacco plugs and whiskey bottles.

8:

The Immigrants

Immigrants were needed by the millions in the 1870s to keep the railroads in ready cash. During that time, railroad agents traveled all over Europe in search of people who were sturdy, healthy, and industrious enough to bear the hard life of settlers in the West, and who also had enough money to make a down payment on railroad land.

To gain the attention of prospective immigrants, the agents opened offices in several European cities and distributed a flood of maps, circulars, and posters. At seaports they boarded ships just before sailing time to make last-minute offers to anyone who might be interested in settling on railroad land.

By the 1880s so many Europeans were leaving for America that several countries tried to discourage their citizens from going. One railroad land agent reported that on a recruiting trip through the Scandinavian countries, some officials treated him like "a robber and a scoundrel of the deepest dye." Another agent traveling in Russia was followed by secret agents of the czar, who did not want the wheat-growing Mennonites to leave Russia for America. Other countries also tried to slow emigration to America by publishing unfavorable accounts of life in the American West, describing it as a land of lawlessness and murder.

Most immigrants who were brought to America by railroad land agents arrived at the port of New York. There they were hustled off their ships into a vast enclosure bearing the romantic name of Castle Garden. Registry clerks then separated them into different nationality groups, recorded their names, countries of origin, and intended destinations. After that the immigrants obtained tickets, checked their baggage, and boarded trains for the West.

On their way across America the immigrants seldom saw any fancy coaches or Pullman cars. Indeed, the railroads which boasted that there were no separate classes of passenger service in democratic America tried to keep immigrants and Pullman passengers out of each other's sight as much as possible. They did not entirely succeed at this, especially at the larger railroad stations, and the general public was so upset by what they saw that in 1873 a bill was introduced in Congress to forbid the railroads to transport human beings as if they were livestock. Nothing much was done, however, to improve the situation.

A traveling Englishwoman told of a sudden meeting with a trainload of immigrants when she stepped off her Pullman car at the Omaha station. "The platform overflows with them, they are everywhere, all with a more or less travel-stained look. Having been penned up so long in such close quarters they are glad to get out and stretch their legs and rinse the dust from their grimy faces. Swarthy men with bare arms are splashing about in buckets or anything that comes handy. The women as a rule look faded, wan, and anxious; the men energetic and strong, confident and assured, with a bright never-say-die look upon their faces. It is a strange gathering, that flock of nationalities, all bound on one adventurous errand—a wave of the Old World breaking on the shores of the new."

Helen Hunt Jackson, an American poet and novelist, described a similar scene of immigrants carrying big bundles and shouting in German, Gaelic, French, and Spanish. "A poor German woman was on her knees before a chest, which had burst open on the journey. It seemed as if the whole contents could not be worth five dollars—so old, so faded, so coarse were the clothes and so battered were the utensils. But it was evidently all she owned; it was the home she had brought with her from the Fatherland, and would be in the home she would set up on the prairie. The railroad men were good to her, and were helping her with ropes and nails. This comforted me somewhat, but it seemed almost a sin to be journeying luxuriously on the same day and train with the poor soul."

In 1879, a twenty-nine-year-old Scottish writer named Robert Louis Stevenson traveled on immigrant cars from New York to California. At that time Stevenson had not become famous as the author of *Treasure Island*, and he did not have enough money to travel by Pullman. He described himself as an "amateur immigrant," viewing his fellow travelers with both sympathy and realism. "They were mostly lumpish fellows, silent and noisy, a common combination; somewhat sad, I should say, with an extraordinary poor taste in humor, and little interest in their fellow creatures beyond that of a cheap and merely external curiosity." Among the foreigners in his car was a German family and "a knot of Cornish miners who kept grimly by themselves, one reading the New Testament all day long through steel spectacles, the rest discussing privately the secrets of their old-world mysterious race."

Stevenson took a violent dislike to a Union Pacific train "butch," a young man who sold newspapers, fruit, and candy to the passengers. He described him as "a dark, bullying, contemptuous, insolent scoundrel, who treated us like dogs." Some days later he almost came to blows with another train butch who kept rudely striking Stevenson's foot whenever he passed in the aisle. But when Stevenson became ill on the train, the butch made him a present of a large juicy pear. "For the rest of the journey I was petted like a sick child. He lent me newspapers, thus depriving himself of his legitimate profit on their sale, and came repeatedly to sit by me and cheer me up."

A PATIENT RAILROAD TRAVELER.

Cartoonist Thomas Nast's depiction of a train butch-or newsboy-
at work.   *(Culver Pictures, Inc.)*

In the car ahead of Stevenson were about fifty Chinese, also bound for California, and he remarked upon the irony of immigrants from hungry Europe and hungry China meeting face to face in the American West. The immigrant cars that Stevenson and his companions rode in were very old coaches—without springs and poorly ventilated—and when in motion they shook and rattled violently. Most of them were worn-out day coaches from Eastern railroads. Some contained double rows of narrow benches without backs and were placed close together so as to squeeze in as many passengers as possible. Usually a coal-burning stove stood at one end of the car, a dangerous fire threat even in a small accident. Passengers traveling in these cars had to sleep on the floor, beneath the benches, or in the aisles.

The transcontinental railroads also introduced immigrant "sleeping cars." They consisted simply of boxlike wooden compartments built one above the other and running along each side of the cars. In these uncurtained boxes the immigrants could lie or sit as they chose, but they had to furnish their own bedding. For some reason, in the West they were called Zulu cars. In the 1880s a few improvements were added. Cooking stoves were placed in the Zulu cars so that immigrants could prepare their own food during the long journey. Wooden straight-backed seats were installed in pairs facing each other so that boards could be placed across them to form beds, and above these seats were slatted sleeping berths supported either by heavy posts or by chains. Upholstery was seldom used in Zulu cars.

Although passengers on immigrant cars were treated as if they were freight instead of human beings, it was the custom to assign men and women to separate cars. Exceptions were sometimes made when large families were traveling together. The train on which Robert Louis Stevenson traveled was segregated also by race, the Chinese being confined to one car.

William Spalding, a young drop-out from the University of Michigan who later became a famous newspaperman, traveled across the West as an immigrant in 1873. He said that he was pleased to be in an all-male car because he "escaped that most intolerable nuisance of miscellaneous traveling, crying babies." There were no

A Zulu car, in which immigrants slept and often prepared their own meals, bound west across the Great Plains.
(*Courtesy of the New-York Historical Society*)

sleeping places on his car, but the seats were made of woven rattan, which made them more comfortable than the usual hard boards. Spalding found that he could stretch out nearly full length in his seat by flexing his knees, and with his overcoat for a pillow and a blanket for covering he somehow survived ten nights of travel.

G. F. Byron, an English immigrant, described the seats on his Zulu car as rough slats with no upholstery. The car had a few wooden cubicles along the sides into which the travelers could climb and stretch out from time to time. For one dollar and twenty-five cents Byron bought a mattress from a railroad agent who told him that he could sell it for the same price when he reached San Francisco. "The mattress was of curious build," Byron wrote, "a flattened square bag of straw, stiff, unwieldy and lumpy, but somehow I managed to force mine into some sort of position, and I certainly found it soothing to sit on."

One of the Zulu cars in which Stevenson rode was fitted so that wooden boards could be placed across the backs of the seats to make a bed. For this he paid two dollars and fifty cents for a board and three straw cushions. Sleep was almost an impossibility, he said, with his fellow travelers sprawled all around him on boards, seats, and flooring. He was continually shaken by the rough motion of the train, and the air was filled with groans and loud complaints.

At journey's end, those immigrants who had been brought to America by a railroad company were usually given temporary shelter in a crude reception house. These houses were built like stations alongside the tracks and were owned by the railroads. They were located near unsold land grants, and agents were waiting there to take the newly arrived immigrants out to choose tracts of land. After making a down payment, they could begin building their future homes in the American West.

9:

From Sherman Summit
to the Golden Gate

Sherman Summit in Wyoming was the halfway point between Omaha and the Union Pacific's end-of-tracks at Ogden, Utah. According to the guidebooks of that time, it was the highest railroad station in the world.

If the westbound express was running on time, the engineer would hold the panting iron horse for a longer than usual stop at the Sherman Summit water tank. This gave the passengers a chance to stretch their legs, inhale the crisp air, and enjoy the view. Soon after starting again, the train crossed the fear-inspiring Dale Creek bridge and plunged down the mountains into Laramie for a noon meal stop.

After lunch at Laramie, where as one traveler said, "the people around the station are more intelligent-looking than at any place since leaving Omaha," the journey continued across the Medicine Bow River. It moved into Carbon Station, where coal had recently been discovered. Coal was important because it was needed to replace wood as fuel on the Union Pacific's locomotives.

Westbound travelers usually crossed Wyoming's deserts after nightfall. Even by moonlight this endless sweep of dry sagebrush and greasewood was described by various observers as being dreary, awful, lifeless. They complained of their burning eyes and sore lips caused by clouds of alkali dust that swirled from the deserts into the cars. Bitter Creek and Salt Wells seemed to be fitting names for stations they passed through.

After sunrise the train arrived at Green River for a breakfast stop. For the next hundred miles the travelers looked forward to the moment the train would cross into the state of Utah. People were curious about the Mormons who lived in Utah, especially about those who practiced polygamy. The idea of having several wives intrigued many of the passengers. The train rumbled into Wahsatch for the noon dining station, and every passenger from the East who stepped down from the train expected to see Mormons. The What Cheer Eating House looked about the same as all the others they had seen, and so did the people there.

A group of people from New England who were traveling on one of the first trains to the West in 1869 were delayed by bad tracks near Wahsatch. One of them did not seem to like the idea of spending the night there. "What a place to stop in! No buildings—nothing but tents or shanties, and all of them 'whiskey hells' of the lowest kinds. We worked our way through the most villainous-looking crowd that man ever set eyes on, to an old sleeping car on a discontinued sidetrack which proved to be densely populated with 'creeping things.' " Wahsatch was filled with several hundred discharged railroad construction workers. They had been paid off by Dr. Durant for the "capture" of his private car, and were busy spending their money in Wahsatch.

"We were afraid they would attack our sleeping car and 'go through it' as the phrase is, and rob the passengers. The ladies were very much frightened; there was very little sleep in the car that night. The doors were securely locked. Some of the party had arms and stood on guard. Many times in the night some of the 'roughs' attempted to get in, and were driven away. They were apparently too drunk to form any organized plan of assault. I did not sleep, and shall long remember those sounds that made the night hideous, of howling, cursing, swearing and pistol shots. Fights occurred by the score; we could distinctly hear the blows. Knives were freely used, and the stabbing affrays were numerous. One man was shot directly under our car window."

About fifty miles farther west, after passing through Echo and Weber canyons, was Uintah Station. This station was a connecting point for Wells, Fargo stagecoaches driving to Salt Lake City. At that time it was considered very fashionable for transcontinental travelers to visit the Mormon capital of Salt Lake City.

Rail travelers from the East were surprised at the beauty of Salt Lake City.   *(Photo by A. J. Russell,*
Courtesy of The Oakland Museum History Department)

Many passengers chose to make the rough thirty-mile stagecoach journey to the Mormon capital. The jarring and jolting was enough "to beat a man into a jelly or to break every bone in his body . . . I am amazed that the wheels and framework of the coach remained unbroken and unstrained."

After the rail spur line from Ogden to Salt Lake City was completed early in 1870 the pilgrimage to the City of the Saints was much easier. When Lady Hardy discovered that the conductor on her train was a Mormon, she immediately asked him how many wives he had. She was surprised by his polite reply that he had only one.

She had thought that the practice of polygamy was required of all men by the Mormon Church.

The city was a pleasant surprise to Easterners whose heads had been filled with anti-Mormon propaganda. "The city, in point of wealth and beauty, far exceeded my expectations," wrote one. "It is a perfect Eden." Another described it as "an oasis in a desert, a blooming garden in a wilderness of green." Almost everyone was entranced by the streams of sparkling water that flowed beside the broad streets. These streams were made from melted snow from the surrounding mountains, and were used to irrigate fields and gardens. One transcontinental tourist, the Finnish Baroness Alexandra Gripenberg, said the Mormons "had done a good piece of work in Utah," and she admired their ability to turn a desert into a garden.

Many travelers criticized the leader of the Mormons, Brigham Young, although those people who met Young in person were impressed by his honesty and abilities. "He exhibited a degree of refinement and intelligence in his discourse which surprised me," said Harvey Rice, who decided the Mormons were "a quiet, orderly people." By the time the transcontinental travelers were back in Uintah or Ogden to continue their trip, most of them had changed their minds about the Mormons.

At Ogden, passengers waiting for connecting trains often had to spend many hours in a long, narrow wooden building. It stood between the tracks of the Union Pacific and the Central Pacific. In addition to ticket offices and a large dining room upstairs, the building had sleeping rooms furnished only with curtains for doors. Lady Hardy thought of her stay in this building as an adventure: "Except for the passing trains this is a most lonely, isolated spot, weird and still, lying in the heart of the mountains. In the evening a blinding snowstorm came on, and the wind, howling fearfully with a rushing mighty sound, shook the doors and rattled at the windows as though it wanted to come in and warm itself at our blazing wood fire."

When they boarded the Central Pacific at Ogden, the first-class passengers found themselves in Silver Palace cars instead of the usual Pullmans. Collis Huntington and his Big Four partners had ordered construction of their own sleeping cars. The Silver Palaces were attractive, with interiors of white metal. They included private sitting rooms and smoking rooms. They were not as luxurious as the Pullman cars, and passengers from the East sometimes complained that the sleeping berths were not as roomy and comfortable. Some said the cars were often too cold. Eventually the Central Pacific had to give up the Silver Palaces because the transcontinental passengers preferred the Pullmans.

The earliest experiment in running a Pullman train from coast to coast was in the spring of 1870. A group of wealthy members of the Boston board of trade was in charge of the journey. George Pullman himself took part, along with 129 members of such leading Boston families as the Rices, Peabodys, Danas, Warrens, Far-

wells, Houghtons, and Whitneys. The Pullman Hotel
Express consisted of two sleeping cars, two hotel cars, a
commissary car, dining car, smoking car, and baggage
car. The smoking car was divided into four compartments. One of these was outfitted with printing presses
for publication of a daily newspaper, *The Transcontinental.* Another compartment had tables for card
games; the others provided areas for a wine room and a
barbershop. The baggage car carried the travel party's
luggage and several chests of ice. Also along for the trip
was a large flask of water from the Atlantic Ocean. The
water was symbolic of the journey from coast to coast.
As special additions to the first luxury train of the future,
Pullman included two libraries and two organs.

Amid considerable newspaper publicity, the Pullman
Hotel Express crossed the continent in seven days. It
stopped only at the larger stations, and meals were
served on board. With much ceremony the flask of symbolic water from the Atlantic was mixed with the water
of the Pacific in San Francisco Bay. After the excursion
was completed, the Union Pacific planned to run the
Hotel Express weekly from Omaha to Ogden. The general public, however, was not yet ready to pay the
added fare for the luxury of the Hotel Express. Perhaps
the financial depression of the early 1870s kept the number of passengers on the luxury train low. After a few
weeks, the service was discontinued. Ten years later,
elegant train travel across the West would become very
popular.

As they rolled westward from Ogden, travelers on the Central Pacific read in their guidebook about the wild towns of Corinne and Promontory. They saw little of those particular towns, though, because the schedule usually brought the train across that part of Utah during the night. In the early months of transcontinental travel, however, Promontory was the transfer stop between the Union Pacific and the Central Pacific. Pioneer journeyers at that time may have seen more of the historic but dying town of Promontory than they wanted.

According to William Humason, who arrived in Promontory a few days after the joining of the rails, the Union Pacific conductor was rude to his passengers. They were told to leave the Union Pacific cars even though there was no Central Pacific train waiting for them. "Out we were turned into the hot sun, with no shade, no hotel, no house—surrounded by no comforts but sand, alkali, and sagebrush. Many of the passengers having had no sleep the night before, looked pretty hard as they sat on their carpet-bags, nodding in the hot sun." There was a hotel in Promontory, called the Pacific, but it was built of wood and canvas. Humason and his New England companions did not go near that shanty-like building or into the gambling dens of that last hell-on-wheels town.

The Cosmopolitan Hotel of booming Elko, Nevada, was the first dining stop west of Ogden. Alkali dust swirled in the streets around freight wagons drawn by long mule teams. The wagons hauled supplies to miners in nearby Pine Valley. Many Chinese lived in Elko, and the travelers would often see them near the hotel. They were former railroad workers who had formed a colony. · Beyond Elko the train passed through the valley of the Humboldt River, and then entered Nevada's deserts. In summer, passengers choked on dust if they left the windows open. They sweltered in heat if they closed them. After passing Winnemucca they turned southward to the Humboldt Sink, where the river seemed to be swallowed up by the desert. Thereafter, instead of facing the sun the iron horse continued a southwesterly course to the Sierras.

By this time the passengers were beginning to show the effects of several days' travel, "a drooping, withered, squeezed-lemon appearance," as one observer put it. "There were the usual crumpled dresses, loose hanging and wayward curls, and ringlets, and *possibly* soiled hands and faces; which reduces the fair sex from that state of perfect immaculateness . . ." Even the independent Susan Coolidge admitted that after two or three days on the Pacific railroad, the dirt and grime made her unhappy. No amount of brushing or shaking could remove the dust from her hair and clothing. One of the common complaints of all early travelers was the discomfort caused by the thick smoke from the locomotives which constantly drifted into the cars.

As the train moved on, the fresh, clean air of the Sierras restored the weary travelers. With two iron horses pulling the cars, the train slowly climbed the winding canyon of the Truckee River. Every mile it climbed eighty feet higher. Pine came into view, replacing the endless desert sagebrush. Farther into the canyon the travelers saw a spectacular view of Donner Lake, circled by mountain forests. The guidebooks usually included stories about the terrible tragedy of the Donner party during the winter of 1846–47. And, "... after snorting and puffing, whistling and screaming, for an hour and a quarter, our pair of iron horses stop in the snowsheds at the station called 'Summit.' Here we have a good breakfast, well cooked and fairly served; although we could not expect waiters enough to attend in a rush such as they have when the passengers, with appetites sharpened by mountain-air and a long ride, seat themselves at table, and all with one voice cry, 'Steak! coffee! bread! trout! waiter! a napkin!' "

The distance from the summit of the Sierras to Sacramento was 105 miles. The track dropped from 7,017 feet to 30 feet above sea level. According to William Humason, 50 miles of the descent was made without using steam. "The conductor and brakeman ran the train with brakes on most of the way." For some travelers this ride down the western slope of the range was terrifying. The coasting trains made so little noise that unwary railroad workers, especially in the snowsheds, often were struck and killed. "The velocity with which the train rushed down this incline, and the suddenness with which it wheeled around the curves," said William Rae, "produced a sensation which cannot be reproduced in words . . . The axle boxes smoked with friction and the odour of burning wood pervaded the cars. The wheels were nearly red hot. In the darkness of the night they resembled discs of flames."

Cape Horn, nine miles below Dutch Flat, was similar to a modern roller coaster. The guidebooks warned timid passengers not to look down when the train passed the awful gorge of the American River. The drop was 2,000 feet. John Beadle said that although Cape Horn offered the finest view in the Sierras, the sight was not good for nervous people. "We're nearing Cape Horn!" someone would always yell and the next moment the train would swing around a sharp curve. "We follow the train around the sides of high mountains," said William Humason, "looking down into a canyon of awful depth, winding around for miles, until we almost meet the track we have before been over—so near that one would think we could almost throw a stone across. We have been around the head of the canyon, and have, therefore, 'doubled Cape Horn.' "

Almost as fascinating as the scenery and the roller-coaster ride were the snowsheds built by engineer Arthur Brown. The sharp sloping roofs of the sheds were built right against the mountainsides. This way, deep snowfalls and avalanches would slide right off the roofs, and drifts were prevented from piling on the railroad tracks. There were so many snowsheds, covering forty miles of track between Truckee and Cape Horn, that passengers complained that the walls blocked their view of the magnificent mountains. The Central Pacific responded to the complaint by cutting windows in the sheds. The windows were placed at the level of the passenger car windows in the train. While it moved along, scenes of the mountains flickered by. Seen through the windows of the train, the scene looked something like an early motion picture. Even this pleasure was denied travelers through the Sierras during the snowiest months of winter because the openings had to be closed. To prevent fires, the Central Pacific kept watchmen inside some of the snowsheds. They had water barrels and hand pumps on hand, ready to put out blazes set off by sparks from the locomotives. There was not much they could do, however, against forest fires when they swept across sections of the sheds. And although the structures were sturdy, a large avalanche might crush one of them. The train on which Lady Hardy was traveling was delayed one night when a shed collapsed. Fifty male passengers helped to clear the tracks.

Besides the main track, snowsheds covered stations, switch tracks, turntables, and the houses where workmen lived with their families. Children who lived in this strange environment had to get used to the dimly lit world where without warning a large boulder or avalanche might crash through their roof. Trains might derail with disastrous results, and on at least one occasion, wild animals escaped from a wrecked circus train. As snowplows were improved, some sheds were taken down. Others were replaced with concrete structures, and gradually the army of workmen became a smaller number of lookouts and track-walkers.

The passage through the Sierras was the first time most of the passengers had seen California. They usually did not feel they were truly in the Golden Land until the iron horse brought them down into the blazing sunshine and balmy air of the Sacramento Valley. Here amid the flowers and orchards of the Queen City of the Plain, "We seem in a new world," said one. "The transition was sudden and the transformation magical," said another. "The sun descended in a flood of glory toward the Pacific Ocean." The travelers were eager to see the coast of the Pacific Ocean, which was still more than a hundred miles away. Until 1870, travelers had to transfer to the California Pacific Railroad to get to Vallejo. From there they changed to a steamboat running down the bay to San Francisco. After the Central Pacific finished building the smaller Western Pacific, the journey became easier. By 1870, the assisting railroad, the Western Pacific, took passengers to Oakland. Travelers still made the final crossing by boat before reaching San Francisco and the ocean. After a week of noise, dust, and locomotive smoke, the first act of many of them would be to register at the magnificent Pacific Hotel. Here they would find a quiet room and a warm bath.

And what were the feelings of travelers after they had completed their first journey by rail across the American continent? People from other countries were usually impressed by the grandeur of the Western land. Of course, many of them compared the American continent with their own nations, sometimes favorably, sometimes unfavorably. Many foreign travelers found the ride by train across the American West to be more fun than a ride by train in their own countries. They could walk about in the cars at their leisure, and could also stand on the platforms and watch the passing landscape.

Yet many of them complained about the lack of privacy on American trains. They enjoyed the comfortable Pullman cars, but did not like to have to transfer from one train to another. Some foreigners also admitted that before starting the journey they had feared the American railroads would not enforce any rules or regulations, and that the locomotives would speed recklessly. They were pleasantly surprised to find that American railway men held human life in as high regard as it was held in their native lands.

American travelers, on the other hand, experienced feelings of national pride. Crossing the vast American West brought out their patriotic emotions as they looked at the prairies, forests, rivers, and towering mountains. It was like seeing a new map unrolled. A new empire was revealed to many Americans, a new civilization in the process of creation. "I felt patriotically proud," wrote one traveler after arriving in California. He thought of the transcontinental railroad as a force binding the United States together, "by links of iron that can never be broken." Americans realized that the first railroad across the nation had been built by private corporations, but they felt that California was a rich prize that had been won for them by those connecting links of iron.

For Americans and foreigners alike, there was a feeling of wonder at this final link in railroad history. In a sense, the world was now encircled by steam power. From San Francisco people could now travel to China and Suez by steam-powered vessels. From Suez they could journey to Alexandria by rail; from Alexandria to France by water; from France to Liverpool by rail and water; from Liverpool to New York by water; and from New York to San Francisco by rail. In reaching the Pacific Ocean, the iron horse had shrunk the planet.

Railroad Terms

ballast: coarse gravel or rocks placed between railroad ties for stability, drainage, and distribution of weight

caboose: the last car on the train, for use by the crew

carriage: passenger car

commissary car: food supply car

conductor: man in charge of the train and the train crew; ticket-taker

coupler or coupling: device for joining cars

engineer:

    1. a person who runs the locomotive, formerly called a "driver"

    2. a person who directs and plans construction of the railroad

fishplate: a piece of metal holding two rails together lengthwise; also called a joint bar

gang: group of railroad workers

grade: to move the ground into a level roadbed

hot boxes: overheated axles

iron horse: locomotive

roadbed: the graded area ready for the rails

sleeper: railroad tie

snowshed: a structure built over the railroad in the mountains, for protection of the rails from snow

spark-arrester: a metal screen to stop burning embers from flying out of the smokestack of wood-burning locomotives

spur: short branch track leading from a railroad's main track, having connection at one end only

surveyor: a person who measures the land for the route of the railroad

switch: a device for moving a train or car from one set of tracks to another

tarrier: Irish railroad laborer

tender: the car directly behind the locomotive, carrying fuel and water

tie: closely spaced wooden beams holding rails evenly apart

track walker: a man who walks and inspects on a certain section of railroad track

turntable: a circular rotating platform used to turn locomotives

vestibuled train: a train with enclosed areas between the passenger cars

Suggested Reading

Alexander, E. P. *Iron Horses, American Locomotives, 1829-1900.* New York: Bonanza Books, 1941.

Athearn, Robert G. *Union Pacific Country.* Chicago: Rand, McNally Co., 1971.

Best, Gerald M. *Iron Horses to Promontory.* San Marino, California: Golden West Books, 1969.

Hirshson, Stanley P. *Grenville M. Dodge: Soldier, Politician, Railroad Pioneer.* Bloomington: Indiana University Press, 1967.

Holbrook, Stewart H. *The Story of American Railroads.* New York: Crown Publishers, 1947.

Howard, Robert West. *The Great Iron Trail.* New York: Bonanza Books, 1962.

Jensen, Oliver. *Railroads in America.* New York: American Heritage Publishing Co., 1975.

Josephson, Matthew. *The Robber Barons.* New York: Harcourt, Brace & World, 1962.

Kinert, Reed. *Early American Steam Locomotives.* New York: Bonanza Books, 1962.

Kraus, George. *High Road to Promontory*. New York: Castle Books, 1969.

Lewis, Oscar. *The Big Four*. New York: Knopf, 1938.

Lyon, Peter. *To Hell in a Day Coach*. Philadelphia: Lippincott, 1968.

McCague, James. *Moguls and Iron Men, the Story of the First Transcontinental Railroad*. New York: Harper & Row, 1964.

Miller, David E., ed. *The Golden Spike*. Salt Lake City: University of Utah Press, 1973.

O'Connor, Richard. *Iron Wheels and Broken Men*. New York: G P. Putnam's Sons, 1973.

Stevenson, Robert Louis. *Across the Plains*. Freeport, New York: Books for Libraries Press, 1972.

Utley, Robert M. and Ketterson, Francis A., Jr. *Golden Spike*. Washington: U.S. National Park Service, 1969.

Index